"AND I WILL BLESS YOU"

Studies in the Abrahamic Covenant

I will make you into a great nation and I will bless you;
I will make your name great, and you will be a blessing.
I will bless those who bless you, and whoever curses you I will curse;
And all peoples on earth will be blessed through you.
Genesis 12:1-3

"And I Will Bless You" - Studies in the Abrahamic Covenant
Copyright© 2014 by HaDavar Messianic Ministries

HaDavar Messianic Ministries
14804 Sand Canyon Avenue
Irvine, CA 92618
Www. HaDavar.org

ISBN-13:978-1499371888
ISBN-10:1499371888
First Edition 2014

Copyright Information

Copyright 2014 © HaDavar Messianic Ministries

Printed in the United States of America

Cover Design by Robert Morris

Artwork from Wikipedia
"The Vision of the Lord Directing Abram to Count the Stars," a woodcut by Julius Schnorr von Carolsfeld from the 1860 *Bible in Pictures.*
"Sarah Laughed" from children's illustrated story.
"Isacc Sacrificed", a woodcut by Julius Schnorr von Carolsfeld from the 1860 *Bible in Pictures*.
"Emblem of Jerusalem," adopted in 1950.

Dedicated to the team, for the glory of God

Susan Morris

Cynthia Esmond

Laura Blasingham

"AND I WILL BLESS YOU"

Studies in the Abrahamic Covenant

TABLE OF CONTENTS

GENESIS 12:1-3
THE PROMISES OF GOD

Will you rely on the promises of God for eternal life,
for your daily walk?

A. INTRODUCTION

In his book, *Encyclopedia of 7,700 Illustrations*, Dr. Paul Tan shares with us this information regarding peace treaties or covenants between nations.

> From the year 1500 BCE to CE 1860 more than 8,000 treaties of peace, meant to remain in force forever, were concluded. The average time they remained in force was two years.[1]

That amazing statistic says something about the reliability of man and his ability to keep a promise.

Covenant keeping lies at the heart of the Bible, at the heart of God, and at the heart of Genesis Chapter 12. In direct contrast to man, God is faithful and He keeps His promises.

Psalm 100:5 tells us:

> For the LORD is good and his love endures forever; His faithfulness continues through all generations.

There are eight covenants or promises outlining God's dealings with man. Chapter 12 of Genesis contains the single most important one of these eight covenants—the Abrahamic

Covenant. It is the single most important promise because from the Abrahamic Covenant flow three other pledges that God has made. This chapter is a critical chapter to know and understand if the rest of the Bible and the rest of this book are going to make sense to us. This is a pivotal chapter around which the entire Bible revolves.

However, before we look into Genesis chapter 12 we need to examine the background of the chapter. The background to the chapter is found in Acts 7:2-4.

B. THE PROMISES OF GOD

Call Issued - Acts 7:2-4

As we look at scripture, it is apparent that God's call to Abraham came to him in two stages.

The call first came to him when he lived with his family in the city of Ur. The city of Ur was located in the region of Chaldea, on the Euphrates River, in southern Mesopotamia. One of the great cities of ancient times, its occupation dates back to about 4000 BCE. Abraham lived there during the period of the Third Dynasty, about 2000 BCE, when the city was at the height of its power and prosperity.[2] At that time, Ur belonged to the most powerful empire in the world. It boasted a highly developed city-civilization, commercial society, and literary culture.[3] Archeology had demonstrated that the area was steeped in polytheistic idolatry.[4]

The original call to Abraham is recorded in the *Brit Chadashah* (New Testament) in Acts 7:2-4. In that chapter, Stephen is defending himself before the Sanhedrin. He begins his defense with these words describing the chronological events surrounding the call to Abraham. Incidentally, the Jewish commentators Ibn Ezra and Radak agree with Stephen's understanding of the sequence of events.[5]

We read in Acts 7:2-4:

> To this he replied: "Brothers and fathers, listen to
> me! The God of glory appeared to our father
> Abraham while he was still in Mesopotamia,
> before he lived in Haran. 'Leave your country and
> your people,' God said, 'and go to the land I will
> show you.' So he left the land of the Chaldeans
> and settled in Haran. After the death of his father,
> God sent him to this land where you are now
> living."

Note that all the power and prosperity of Ur at the height of its
glory did not prevent Abraham from following God's call. To do
the will of God was more important to him than the riches of this
world.

Abraham's response to this first call regarding his sojourn to
Haran is recorded in Genesis 11:31-32:

> Terah took his son Abram, his grandson Lot son
> of Haran, and his daughter-in-law Sarai, the wife
> of his son Abraham, and together they set out
> from Ur of the Chaldeans to go to Canaan. But
> when they came to Haran, they settled there.
> Terah lived 205 years, and he died in Haran.

In response to God's call, Abraham's entire family left Ur of the
Chaldees and made the 600 mile trek to Haran in northern
Mesopotamia. Their original destination was the land of Canaan.
However, they never got there. Once Abraham's father got to
Haran, he chose to settle down in that city instead of continuing
on. Whatever his reason for doing so, this was as far as Terah
wanted to go with God. So Abraham's beginning with God has
started out on a rather shaky basis.

On the positive side, Abraham has obeyed. He has left his
country of Chaldea, he has left his people - his friends and

relatives, and he has started out for the land promised by God.

However, on the negative side, the obedience is half-hearted. The influence of Abraham's father, Terah, has stopped Abraham from continuing on to the land that God had promised. At the moment, compromise and hesitation has crippled Abraham's obedience. He started out on a new life of faith and obedience, but now he is holding back or he is being held back from fully following through. He is wasting years in Haran.

However, God is not finished with Abraham yet. The call of God is heard once again in Genesis 12:1.

Abraham's Second Call – Genesis 12:1a

Genesis 12:1a tells us:

> The LORD had said to Abram, "Leave your country, your people and your father's household…"

God's call comes again, but now it includes a third element. In Ur, the call contained two aspects. "Leave your country and your people." Now, when the call comes again, a third requirement is added. "…and (leave) your father's household." The influence of his immediate family is what has been holding Abraham back. Now, Abraham replaced his compromise with commitment. He replaced his hesitation with obedience, and he did what God was asking him to do.

There is always a negative side and a positive side to following the call of God.

Genesis 12:1a highlights the negative side of obedience. Abraham had to leave behind his old life entirely. His whole being was involved in this decision of faith. The whole man was involved -- body, soul, and spirit.

He was told to "leave your country." This deals with the physical involvement of his body. We all know that moving is a hard thing to do. Abraham had to pack his bags, pull up stakes, and physically move out. He had to move not just down the block but to an entirely new country and culture and way of life. He had to leave behind the old life in Ur. He had to physically leave a country that did not value God. It is hard to leave your country where you have all your associations, but Abraham was willing to do that.

Next, Abraham was told to "leave his people." This speaks of the commitment in his soul; his mind, his will, and his emotions were impacted by this call. He had to leave behind the old companionships, the old supports, and the old ways of thinking. He had to mentally and emotionally leave friends that did not value God. It is hard to leave your country, but it is harder still to leave your people -- your relatives and friends, but Abraham was willing to do that.

Finally, he was told to "leave his father's house." This speaks of the commitment of his spirit. Abraham could not let his immediate family become an idol in his life. He could not let his father's house come between him and God. His father was not willing to go all the way with God. So Abraham was faced with a choice. Which do I follow, God or my father? The death of his father, Terah, provided the nudge he needed to make this final and most difficult decision. Abraham had to leave behind those in his immediate family who did not value God. His close family would now be limited to those people who trusted God with the same intensity that he had. It is hard to leave your country; it is harder still to leave your people. It is most difficult of all to leave that most cherished of all relationships, your intimate family circle. Abraham's toughest decision was to leave his family who meant so much to him, but this is what Abraham finally was willing to do.[6]

He finally chose to lean upon God body, soul, and spirit -- he held nothing back. Your country, your people, and your father's house are the main influences which mold a person's thoughts and actions. This call indicates the severity of the trial which was being asked of him. This was no small, casual decision that Abraham was being asked to make. He was to cut himself completely adrift from all associations that could possibly hinder his walk with God.[7] All these associations had roots that went down to the very bottom of his soul. This is the negative side of God's call.

The positive side begins in the second half of verse 1 and continues on into verses 2 and 3.

C. COVENANT INSTITUTED

Land – Genesis 12:1b

Verse 12:1b says:

> ...and go to the land I will show you.

The positive side of the call begins with the word "land." God called Abraham out of his present country not to cause him hardship or to set him adrift on the sea of life. God called Abraham out of his old land in order to give him a new country, and a new home, and a new beginning.[8] The first provision of the Abrahamic Covenant is a land. That land is not identified at this time. Its borders are not explained, but nevertheless, it is Abraham's land.

The second provision of the Abrahamic Covenant is explained in the first part of verse 2.

Nation (seed) – Genesis 12:2a

We learn from 12:2a:

> I will make you into a great nation...

The next promise is that of a nation. A nation will dwell in this land that God is giving to Abraham. God has given a country back to Abraham. Now He is giving him back a people. God is promising Abraham that from his body a nation will emerge and that nation will be great. This does not mean numerical greatness. In Deuteronomy 7:7, God said that Israel was "the fewest of all peoples." The Jewish people have never been the most populous nation in the world. The worldwide Jewish population today only numbers some 14.5 million people.[9] The Jewish people have a long way to go before they equal China's 1.3 billion people,[10] or even the U.S.A.'s 295 million people.[11] Israel's greatness will not lie in the area of land that it covers or in the size of the population.

Israel's true greatness has always been spiritual in nature. Israel's greatness has always been found in God's revelation of Himself to her and in His choice of Israel to preserve that revelation for the world. The tremendous force of this promise to Abraham lies in the fact that when it was first made, Abraham was 75 years old and had no son. No descendants, not a single one had yet emerged from Abraham's body.

God has promised Abraham a land and a people. He has given back to Abraham a land and a people. Now He moves on to the third provision of the Covenant, the second phrase of verse 2.

Blessings – Genesis 12:2b

Verse 2b says:

> ...and I will bless you;

This promise refers primarily to Abraham himself. God blessed Abraham personally from the day Abraham believed God's word and committed himself to a life of faith and obedience. From that time on, God increasingly revealed Himself to Abraham in a person to person relationship. Abraham came to understand that God was the one who loved him and took responsibility for his welfare. For example, in Genesis 12 and 13, God personally talked with Abraham. In Genesis 15, Abraham came to know God as His shield and as his "very great reward." God is the one who gave to Abraham the deepest desires of his heart.

God eventually and miraculously gave him his son, Isaac. Essentially, what God is giving back to Abraham is a new family. He will act as Abraham's father and provide Abraham with an abundant life. God gives back to Abraham all that He asked him to renounce in the beginning. God gives back to Abraham a country, a people and a household.

However, all that Abraham has at this moment in time are promises and nothing more. He only grasps abstract, immaterial words. He does not even know where he is going. He holds nothing concrete in his hands. He has to trust God for the fulfillment and the reality of these promises.

The blessings that Abraham would receive are both temporal and spiritual in nature. The first temporal blessing is, of course, the land itself. This is repeated in Genesis 13:14-15:

> The LORD said to Abram after Lot had parted from him, "Lift up your eyes from where you are and look north and south, east and west. All the land that you see I will give to you and your offspring forever."

Eretz Yisrael (the land of Israel) was personally given to Abraham and to his descendants.

Another temporal blessing that God gave to Abraham was wealth. In Genesis 24:35, Abraham's servant describes his master with these words:

> The LORD has blessed my master abundantly, and he has become wealthy. He has given him sheep and cattle, silver and gold, menservants and

maidservants, and camels and donkeys.

These are some of the temporal blessings that Abraham received, but spiritual blessings are also included in this promise. The most important is the promise of salvation from sin. Genesis 15:6 tells us:

> Abram believed the LORD, and he credited it to him as righteousness.

The basis of spiritual salvation is the same for every person in every age. The basis of salvation for Abraham and for anyone else is this: salvation comes by God's grace through faith, through trusting plus nothing else.[12] When we place our trust in God, then God responds out of His love and mercy. He responds out of His grace and He gives us the gift of eternal life.

Now, the content of faith varies from age to age. In Abraham's case, he placed his faith in the promises of God. He trusted that God would fulfill all these promises to him. In our case, in our day and age, we place our trust in the God/Man. We trust in *Yeshua* (Jesus) and His work on our behalf. The content of faith may vary, but the trust or the faith is the same for everybody. This is the first spiritual blessing that Abraham received.

Abraham was also given a glimpse of the Messiah and the Messianic Kingdom. In John 8:56, *Yeshua* said these words about Abraham:

> Your father Abraham rejoiced at the thought of seeing my day; he saw it and was glad.

How much information about the Messiah and the Messianic Kingdom God revealed to His friend Abraham is unknown. But it is clear that he knew something of the coming Messiah and of the coming Messianic Kingdom, and he rejoiced in knowing about it and expecting it. This is another spiritual blessing that he received.

The next aspect of the Covenant is discovered as verse 2 continues.

Personal Honor – Genesis 12:2c

We are told in verse 2c:

> I will make your name great...

Again, God personally blesses Abraham, this time with honor and glory. His name, indeed, is one of the great names of all history. The very fact that we are reading about him in the pages of sacred scripture at this very moment attests to this truth. Abraham's greatness can be seen in some of the other descriptive names he was given.

In Genesis 17:5, he is called the "father of many nations."

In Genesis 23:6, he is called "a mighty prince."

In Genesis 20:7, he is called "a prophet."

In Isaiah 41:8, he is called "my (God's) friend."

And in Galatians 3:9, he is called "the man of faith."

This promise from God, personal honor and glory, has indeed come to pass.

At this point, God turns from dealing personally with Abraham and begins to explain how Abraham will affect others.

Abraham's Responsibility – Genesis 12:2d

In verse 12:2d we learn:

> ...and you will be a blessing.

The consequence or the result that will flow from God making Abraham great is that he will be a blessing to others. God did not promise all this to Abraham so that he could selfishly hoard it for himself or that he could proudly look down his nose at everyone else and say, "God loves me, look how great I am." God exalted Abraham for this reason: so that Abraham would be a source of abundant living for others.

To bless someone in Biblical thinking means to empower them and to enable others to experience success and prosperity. Abraham was to enable others to possess an abundant life. Abraham was now under the moral obligation. He was under moral responsibility to share his life and to see to it that his life benefited others.

God had outlined Abraham's relationship with others. Now God explains what His relationship will be to those who surround Abraham in the first half of verse 3.

God's Responsibility – Genesis 12:3a

We learn from 12:3a:

> I will bless those who bless you, and whoever curses you I will curse...

This aspect of the Abrahamic Covenant is a two-edged sword with positive and negative stipulations. God takes on an offensive and defensive responsibility for Abraham's welfare.[13]

God begins with the positive aspect of the promise. God promises Abraham that He will personally identify with Abraham and his descendants. He and Abraham will be so closely connected that for anyone to be kind, good, or generous to Abraham would be considered as being kind, good, and generous toward God Himself. Anyone who benefits Abraham and his descendants will experience prosperity and an abundant life from God.

Then God flips over the coin and begins to deal with the negative side of the promise. Now He says, "...and whoever curses you I will curse." The thought of the phrase is that Abraham will be so identified with God that to deliberately curse Abraham is almost equivalent to cursing God.

The word "curse" used here means "to bind, to hem in with obstacles, to render powerless to resist."[14] Whoever seeks the hinder Abraham, to block him, to render him powerless, to destroy his quality of life, will be blocked and hemmed in and rendered powerless themselves.

The principle that God operates on is summed up in this phrase: blessing for blessing in kind and curse for curse in kind. Throughout history this principle has continued to operate in regard to Abraham's seed, the nation of Israel. God will promote the welfare of whoever seeks the welfare of the Jewish people.

An example centering on the Roman Centurion is found in Luke 7:2-5:

> There a centurion's servant, whom his master valued highly, was sick and about to die. The centurion heard of Jesus and sent some elders of the Jews to him, asking him to come and heal his servant. When they came to Jesus, they pleaded earnestly with him, "This man deserves to have you do this, because he loves our nation and has built our synagogue."

During the first century the Romans were hardly the friends of the Jewish people. However, there is something different about this particular Roman soldier. He loves the Jewish people and he seeks their welfare. As a result, *Yeshua* honors this Gentile's faith and promotes the welfare of his household by healing his servant. Why? It is because of his relationship with the Jewish people and the promise of blessing for blessing in kind.

However, there is another edge to the sword. Whenever people or nations unjustly afflict the Jewish people, they have invariably suffered.[15]

When Egypt afflicted the Jewish people and tried to kill all her first born sons by drowning them, they experienced retribution in two stages. The first stage was during the events of the Exodus when God sent the 10th plague upon Egypt with the death of their first born sons, curse for curse in kind. Stage two happens when Israel left Egypt. The Egyptian army chased them in hot pursuit, and so God destroyed the Egyptian army by drowning them, curse for curse in kind.

No sooner than Israel left Egypt than another nation comes to curse the Jews.

In Exodus 17:8 we read:

> The Amalekites came and attacked the Israelites at Rephidim.

The curse employed against Israel here is war. Amalek declared war on Israel, and so God declares war on Amalek. That is why King Saul is commanded later to attack and obliterate the Amalekites.

In the book of Esther, Haman sets out with his curse against the Jews. Because one Jew, Mordechai, refuses to bow down to him, Haman wants to destroy all the Jews. He personally wants to kill Mordechai by hanging him on his very own gallows. However, God goes to work and in the end, it is Haman that swings from the gallows, not Mordechai, curse for curse in kind.

In modern times, the same pattern is followed in the case of Spain, England and Germany. At one time, each of these nations treated the Jewish people with favor and respect and they benefited. Spain had her empire, England hers, and Germany experienced prosperity. However, each of these nations also turned against the Jewish people. Spain and England both lost their far flung empires, and Germany was crushed in the events of WW2, curse for curse in kind.

In the future, the world will witness this principle fall in a most dramatic manner on the nation of Russia. Someday Russia will choose to invade Israel leading a coalition of armies. She will be brought to her knees by the direct intervention from God Himself, curse for curse in kind.[16]

God has so chosen to identify with the seed of Abraham that to bless or curse the Jewish people brings blessing or cursing from God Himself.

The final aspect of the Abrahamic Covenant is revealed in the last part of verse 3.

Extent - Genesis 12:3b

Genesis 12:3b says:

> ...and all peoples on earth will be blessed through you.

This statement explains the extent of the Abrahamic Covenant. It tells how far it reaches. God has a plan of blessing that includes all the nations of the world. That plan was to be realized through Abraham and his seed.[17] This is the promise that crowned all the rest; for it points at the Messiah.[18]

This promise is a promise of spiritual blessings, a promise that the Gentiles are included in God's salvation program. This aspect of the Abrahamic Covenant finds its fulfillment in the fact that Jesus became the means of blessing to the world (Gal. 3:8, 16; cf. Rom. 9:5).[19]

This truth is explained succinctly for us by Rabbi Shaul in his letter to the Messianic congregations in Galatia. He says in Galatians 3:8-9:

> The Scripture foresaw that God would justify the Gentiles by faith, and announced the gospel in advance to Abraham: "All nations will be blessed through you." So those who have faith are blessed

along with Abraham, the man of faith.

Genesis 12:3 is foretelling that the spiritual blessing of justification by faith will extend beyond Abraham to the entire world. Gentiles who trust God and His promises receive the exact same blessing that Abraham received, righteous standing before God.

Rabbi Shaul also says in Galatians 3:14:

> He redeemed us in order that the blessing given to Abraham might come to the Gentiles through Christ Jesus, so that by faith we might receive the promise of the Spirit.

This statement tells us why God is saving Gentiles, the very reason why God is grafting in Gentiles. It is in fulfillment of His promise to Abraham, the promise made in Genesis 12:3. With this, the inconceivable promises of the Abrahamic Covenant come to a close.

Before we come to the application, let us quickly summarize the Abrahamic Covenant. If you strip it down to its basics, the Abrahamic Covenant consists of three blessings - land blessings, nation blessings and spiritual blessings.

What we have in Genesis 12:1-3 are the bare bones, just the skeleton of that promise. As we continue through scripture, God progressively fleshes out these three blessings so that we can see them in their full glory. As we go through scripture, what we learn is this:

The land blessings are expanded and developed through the Land Covenant of Deuteronomy 29 and 30. The nation blessings are expanded and developed in the Davidic Covenant of 2 Samuel 7 and 1 Chronicles 17. Finally, the spiritual blessings are expanded and developed in the New Covenant of Jeremiah 31 (see chart on following page).

THE ABRAHAMIC COVENANT Eternal and Unconditional	Land Promise (Israel) ✿ To You ✿ To Your Descendents	Land Covenant Deut 29-30
	National Promise ✿ National Election ✿ Unique Relationship w/ Gentile Nations	Davidic Covenant 2 Sam 7:10-17 1 Chron 17:10-15 Ps 89:1-4, 19-37
	Spiritual Blessing Promise ✿ I will bless you. ✿ You will bless others	New Covenant Jer 31-31-34 Ezekiel 36:24-28

These three additional covenants are the flowers that bloom upon the stem of the Abrahamic Covenant. We can see why Abraham and the Abrahamic Covenant play such a pivotal role in the God's revelation to man.

Around this one trusting heart, God has constructed a program that reaches out to every man and woman who has lived or will ever live on the face of this planet.

D. APPLICATION

The passage teaches us that genuine faith obeys God.

Abram was middle-aged, prosperous, and had settled in Ur of the Chaldees. Then the word of the LORD came to Him, and he responded in faith. He obediently left everything to follow God's plan. His departure to a new life required an unparalleled act of faith[20] -- of trust. That is why he is the epitome of faith in the Bible.[21]

A similar call comes to Abraham's physical and spiritual descendants in every age and time, to separate themselves from all associations and influences that are harmful to their faith and destiny.[22]

This call comes to us, as well. We are not to become hermits in wilderness caves, but we are to live righteous lives in the world and glorify God by blessing other people. We do this on the basis of faith. We do this on the basis of trusting God. He asks us to renounce the certainties of the past and face the uncertainties of the future by looking for and following His direction.[23]

Are you ready to make a new beginning like Abraham did? Are you ready to say good bye to your old life and move out on a new life, walking in a close relationship with God? Are you willing to trust in the great and precious promises that He offers to all who trust in Him?

He offers two basic promises. 1) The promise of eternal life, and 2) The promise that He will never leave you nor forsake you no matter what comes your way. Would you like to be blessed this way and in turn be a blessing to others? These promises are received on the basis of trusting God.

Abraham was just a man. If he can do it, then we can do it.

Will you rely on the promises of God for eternal life and for your daily walk?

GENESIS 18:1-15
THEY LAUGHED

The LORD wants us to trust in His very great and precious promises because they are guaranteed by His perception and His power

A. INTRODUCTION

The *Torah* portion before us is Genesis 18:1-15. The background of this chapter is the Abrahamic Covenant. God called Abraham out of his home in Ur of the Chaldees and told him to go to a new land. In a magnificent act of faith, in an extraordinary act of trust, Abraham obeyed. When he arrived in the land, God entered into a covenant relationship with him. That covenant, for convenience sake, we call the Abrahamic Covenant. It is found in Genesis 12:1-3. At that time, when Abraham was just slightly beyond 75 years of age, God made three basic promises. God promised him a land, God promised him spiritual blessings, and God promised him descendants. The last promise is the one that we focus in on today—the promise of a child. And not only a child but an entire nation would spring from Abraham.

The years passed and it appeared that God might not fulfill His promise that Abraham would have descendants. In the 16th chapter of Genesis, when Abraham is now 85 years old, Sarah, his wife, was convinced that the LORD had deliberately withheld children from her. She tries to fulfill God's promise for Him; she tries to help God out by giving Abraham her servant girl as his second wife. Soon, Ishmael is born, but Sarah and Abraham both knew in their hearts that this was not the child that God had promised. Ishmael was the child of human effort, not the child of Divine pledge. In the 17th chapter of Genesis, when Abraham is now 99 years old, God appears to him confirming the promise He made 24 years earlier. The confirmation of the promise comes in Genesis 17:16. Regarding Sarah, God says to Abraham:

> I will bless her and will surely give you a son by
> her. I will bless her so that she will be the mother
> of nations; kings of peoples will come from her.

The reaction of Abraham to this confirmation was faith and rejoicing. In Genesis 17:17-18 we read that Abraham fell facedown; he laughed and said to himself:

> Will a son be born to a man a hundred years old?
> Will Sarah bear a child at the age of ninety?

He is not doubting God here, he is marveling, he is astounded. The promise was so immensely great that he sank to the ground in adoration. The promise was so incredibly impossible that he was filled with wonder and he burst into laughter.[24]

Romans 4:18-21 describes Abraham's reaction with these words:

> Against all hope, Abraham in hope believed and
> so became the father of many nations, just as it
> had been said to him, "So shall your offspring be."
> Without weakening in his faith, he faced the fact
> that his body was as good as dead—since he was
> about a hundred years old—and that Sarah's
> womb was also dead. Yet he did not waver
> through unbelief regarding the promise of God,
> but was strengthened in his faith and gave glory to
> God, being fully persuaded that God had power to
> do what he had promised.

Abraham possessed faith and trust in God's sovereign, unlimited power. In Genesis 17:19 God tells Abraham what to name this child of promise:

> Then God said, "Yes, … your wife Sarah will bear
> you a son, and you will call him Isaac …"

The name that Abraham will give his son means literally in the Hebrew, "he will laugh."[25] God deliberately chose the name so that it would be a constant reminder of Abraham's immense faith and trust. Every time he uttered the name of his son, he would be reminded of the day that God confirmed His promise, of the day that Abraham laughed for joy. Abraham's laughter was very significant; it revealed his inner attitude of trust.

Now we are ready for Chapter 18. In this chapter someone else will laugh in a very significant way, revealing their inner attitude as well, and so this chapter is entitled "They Laughed."

As we study this section of Holy Scripture, we will learn that the LORD wants us to trust in His very great and precious promises because they are guaranteed by His perception and His power.

At this point we are ready to start our examination of Genesis 18:1-15. Our study of God's Promise begins with His appearance to Abraham in verses 1 and 2.

B. GOD'S PROMISE

Appearance - Genesis 18:1-2

> The LORD appeared to Abraham near the great
> trees of Mamre while he was sitting at the
> entrance to his tent in the heat of the day.

Verse 1 provides us with the setting, and verse 1 is the key to the entire section. This verse clarifies the significance of this incident right from the start.

Abraham has set up his tent in the shade afforded by this grove of trees growing in the district called Mamre. Mamre is located about 20 miles south of Jerusalem. It is very close to the modern

city of Hebron. The key to understanding the incident before us is
then clearly stated in verse 1:

Now the LORD appeared to Abraham ...

The personal name of God is used here, the yud-hay-vav-hay
(יְהוָה[26])This is an appearance of God Himself; this is no
messenger, no angel, no substitute. This is the real thing. The
form that the invisible God takes as He makes Himself visible to
Abraham is described in verse 2:

> Abraham looked up and saw three men standing
> nearby. When he saw them, he hurried from the
> entrance of his tent to meet them and bowed low
> to the ground.

Three men appear to Abraham. The Artscroll Tenach
commentary suggests that this was totally unexpected. This
Orthodox Jewish commentary states:

> ...the men had not approached from afar, but
> were suddenly standing there as though
> materializing from thin air.[27]

In other words, the form that God takes upon Himself is a human
form. God, Himself, is one of these three men. The other two
individuals are angels, also in human form. Abraham seems to
clearly understand the heavenly nature of these visitors.[28] Would
not we bow down as well if suddenly somebody appeared out of
thin air in front of us?

For God to appear in human form is seen in other sections of the
Bible. God can do anything He chooses to do since He is all
powerful. This is something He is quite capable of doing and
something He has done before. When He chooses to reveal
Himself in a form that we can see, He sometimes wraps Himself
in fire. Sometimes He wraps Himself in a cloud. Here, He wraps
a human form around His invisible, spirit nature.

Abraham was not the only one to see God in human form. The prophet Ezekiel also saw God in human form in Ezekiel 1:26-28:

> Now above the expanse that was over their heads there was something resembling a throne, like lapis lazuli in appearance; and on that which resembled a throne, high up, was a figure with the appearance of a man. Then I noticed from the appearance of His loins and upward something like glowing metal that looked like fire all around within it, and from the appearance of His loins and downward I saw something like fire; and there was a radiance around Him. As the appearance of the rainbow in the clouds on a rainy day, so was the appearance of the surrounding radiance. Such was the appearance of the likeness of the glory of the LORD. And when I saw it, I fell on my face and heard a voice speaking.

In this encounter with Ezekiel, not only did the LORD wrap Himself in a human form, but He added to that form with fire and radiance and color. Abraham's experience was much more sedate. The human form was there, but not the fire and the glory and the colors.

Two thousand years later, God would clothe Himself in this form once again in John 1:1:

> In the beginning was the Word, and the Word was with God, and the Word was God.

In John 1.14 it says:

> And the Word became flesh, and made his dwelling among us. We have seen his glory, the glory of the One and Only, who came from the Father, full of grace and truth.

The *Brit Chadashah* (New Covenant) testifies that God did this very same thing when He walked among us in the person of our Messiah. The *Brit Chadashah* testifies that when men looked upon *Yeshua* (Jesus), they looked upon God Himself clothed in human form.

Attitude – Genesis 18:3-5

Abraham's attitude toward his three heavenly visitors is revealed in Genesis 18:3-5:

> He said, "If I have found favor in your eyes, my Lord, do not pass your servant by. Let a little water be brought, and then you may all wash your feet and rest under this tree. Let me get you something to eat, so you can be refreshed and then go on your way—now that you have come to your servant." "Very well," they answered, "do as you say."

Abraham's attitude was one of reverent humility. He speaks to one of the men, and only one according to the form of the Hebrew used. He calls that individual "Adonai", (אֲדֹנָי[29]) LORD. According to three sources, the Artscroll Tenach Commentary, *Jewish Halachah* (Jewish law), and the position of the rabbi's, Adonai is the name that refers to God.[30] Let us repeat that. According to the rabbi's, the word Adonai is sacred, and it refers to God. The Artscroll Tenach Commentary quotes the two respected Jewish commentators, Rashi and Rambam, in support of this position. In other words, Abraham is speaking to God here, God appearing in human form. That is the plain meaning of the text.

In reverent humility Abraham offers his heavenly guests typical Middle Eastern hospitality. They accept his generosity, and he launches into action.

Action – Genesis 18:6-8

> So Abraham hurried into the tent to Sarah. "Quick," he said. "Get three seahs of fine flour and knead it and bake some bread." Then he ran to the herd and selected a choice, tender calf and gave it to a servant, who hurried to prepare it. He then brought some curds and milk and the calf that had been prepared, and set these before them. While they ate, he stood near them under a tree.

We are justified in seeing some great lessons on hospitality in these three verses. Abraham was eager to share with others; he hurried as he gathered the food. He was personally involved in the preparations. He was generous. His comments indicate that he prepared a more than ample meal. He gave of his best. The bread was made from the choicest flour he had available, and the calf was the finest his herd could offer. He was attentive. He stood by his guests as they ate. He was ready to fulfill their every wish.

These are all lessons that we should apply to our lives as well. We are commanded in Romans 12:13 and 1 Peter 4:9 to pursue hospitality with the same eagerness that Abraham did. Hospitality to each other[31], to strangers[32], to the poor[33] and even to our enemies[34] should mark our lives as believers. Because God has shared all of His good things with us, we should be willing to share our good things with others. We need to be willing to refresh others and care for their needs.

Abraham was everything a good, Middle Eastern host should be. He was eager, personally involved, generous and attentive. He was everything, everything that is, except rabbinically kosher. If you will notice in verse 8, he served milk and meat together. The plain meaning of the text indicates that Abraham served the milk and meat at the same time. Serving milk and meat together is not part of the biblical food laws, but it is part of the rabbinic traditions. The rabbi's, of course, noticed this. Those rabbi's who stick with the plain meaning of the text acknowledge Abraham's breech of their tradition. Those who wish to make Abraham into a rabbi interpret the text to make it line up with rabbinic tradition. There are obvious conflicting rabbinic opinions regarding this issue.[35]

Of course, the whole controversy is really a non-issue when you consider the fact that neither the Mosaic Laws nor rabbinic laws were in existence at this time. Abraham didn't break any laws of Kashrut because there were not any laws of Kashrut during his day and age.

When you get right down to it, teaching lessons about hospitality and the laws of Kashrut are not the reasons why the heavenly visitors came to Abraham. That is not the point of the text. The reason why they came becomes apparent in the affirmation that follows in verses 9 and 10

Affirmation – Genesis 18:9-10

> "Where is your wife Sarah?" they asked him. "There, in the tent," he said. Then the LORD said, "I will surely return to you about this time next year, and Sarah your wife will have a son." Now Sarah was listening at the entrance to the tent, which was behind them.

The entire scene before us speaks of God's intimate love and personal relationship with his friend[36] Abraham. To eat together in that culture meant far more than it does in our society today. This was no quick business lunch between God and Abraham. In that culture to eat together meant that the persons who ate and drank were bound to one another by friendship and mutual obligation.[37] Meals often marked events of special significance.[38]

That is exactly what we have here. In verse 10 we see the

primary reason why God Himself came to visit Abraham. He came to pinpoint for Abraham the exact timing for the fulfillment of His promise.[39] God, in His own gentle, loving, personal way comes to fellowship with His friend and let him know exactly when he will hold his newborn son in his arms. Nothing could more significantly communicate their close relationship.[40]

Verse 10 also sets the scene for Sarah's reaction to this incredible promise. Verse 10 tells us that Sarah stands close by within hearing distance. She is listening intently to all that is going on, but she is off camera. She is in the tent behind the speaker. The speaker cannot see her, and from His comments, apparently He has no idea where she is. She thinks that she is anonymous and invisible to her guests. But she is wrong, dead wrong. The misconception regarding her guests is about to be exploded.

C. GOD'S PERCEPTION

Adversity - Genesis 18:11

> Abraham and Sarah were already old and well
> advanced in years, and Sarah was past the age of
> childbearing.

Verse 11 explains to us the problem, the adversity, the obstacle that blocked the fulfillment of God's promise. The problem was old age. The primary obstacle to the fulfillment of God's promise was Sarah's age. The Artscroll Tenach Commentary states that the Hebrew expression used to describe her is used to describe someone upon whom old age weighs heavily. It describes one upon whom life has taken its toll.[41]

She was ninety years old. Sarah, as with all women her age, was no longer physically capable of even conceiving a child. Why, we should ask, why in the world would God allow this to happen? Why in the world would God make a promise and then bring it to the brink of failure?[42]

There is a reason for all this. God has allowed the obstacles to grow great enough in order to demonstrate that the promise, when fulfilled, would come from Him alone.

Sarah's reaction and attitude regarding what she heard is revealed in verse 12.

Attitude - Genesis 18:12

> So Sarah laughed to herself as she thought, "After I am worn out and my master is old, will I now have this pleasure?"

Sarah laughed silently in her heart. This was not an audible laugh. Nobody physically heard this chuckle with their ears. However, it revealed what she thought of herself, and what she thought of the situation, and what she though of the promise.

Regarding herself, she sees herself as worn out. The Hebrew word is used of clothes that are in tatters.[43] She compares herself to an old threadbare rag that is ready to be tossed away as useless, unneeded, and unwanted.

In regard to the situation, the circumstances were inconceivable (pun intended). Bearing a child was a pleasure she consigned to the scrap heap of life decades ago.

In regard to the promise, it was impossible to be fulfilled. The promise consisted of empty words without substance or meaning, full of disappointment and delusion. Hers was a silent laugh full of bitterness and irritation and disappointment. She thought it was a private laugh. She thought that her helplessness and hopelessness and depression were only known to herself. This was her attitude as she stood at the entrance of her tent and listened silently to the conversation before her. It was an attitude of disbelief as well as dreary, dismal, discouragement. God's promise was a farce, a fraud, a fake. Little did she know that there was someone there who perceived what was going on inside her soul. There was someone there who knew all about the distress and discouragement that lay heavy upon her. That perception and knowledge is revealed in Genesis 18:13:

> Then the LORD said to Abraham, "Why did Sarah laugh and say, 'Will I really have a child, now that I am old?'"

In verse 13 God Himself speaks up. This is the LORD Himself. God's personal name, yud-hey-vav-hey, is present in the text. What did God do here? God read her mind. God perceived the thoughts and intents of her heart. God asks Abraham this question, not out of ignorance because He already knew the answer to the question. He asks this question for the purpose of revealing to Abraham the fact that He knows all that is going on. Our mighty God is all-knowing and nothing catches Him by surprise. He perceives everything, even the thoughts inside our heads.

Jeremiah 17:10 reads:

> I, the LORD, search the heart, I test the mind, Even to give to each man according to his ways, according to the results of his deeds.

This ability to perceive all that goes on, this ability to know our thoughts, is a characteristic reserved for God alone. No one else has this ability. For example, Solomon prays in 2 Chronicles 6:30:

> ...deal with each man according to all he does, since you know his heart (for you alone know the hearts of men), ...

Once we understand this, once we understand God's ability to perceive, then certain incidents in the life of the Messiah take on new significance. Whenever you read the accounts of the Messiah's life, pay careful attention to the times that *Yeshua* reads peoples' minds. Note those occasions that contain statements like this one in Matthew 9:4:

> And *Yeshua* knowing their thoughts said, "Why are you thinking evil in your hearts?"

And this one from Mark 2:8:

> Immediately Jesus, aware in His spirit that they were reasoning that way within themselves, said to them, "Why are you reasoning about these things in your hearts?"

Do you see the parallel between these statements and the event in Genesis 18:13? The exact same thing is happening. God in human form is walking among men and revealing who He is by perceiving their thoughts. Every time *Yeshua* did this, those who knew their Bible would immediately recall what happened in Genesis 18. Every time *Yeshua* did this, it revealed His Divine nature. This ability revealed that He was the God-man. It was a claim to be God in human form because only God has the ability to perceive our thoughts. In fact, the one who is speaking to Abraham in Genesis 18 is the pre-incarnate Messiah. Abraham is talking to God the Son. This is why *Yeshua* could say in John 8:56:

> Your father Abraham rejoiced to see My day, and he saw it and was glad.

As God asks Abraham the question in verse 13, there is probably great tenderness and sadness in His voice. God may know everything, but He is also a person who desires our love and trust. He does not force us to love Him or trust Him. All of us make the deliberate and free and responsible decision to love Him and to trust Him or to doubt Him and reject Him. Even though He knows our hearts, it still brings Him pain when we do not trust Him and love Him. Mankind is still free and responsible even though God is all-knowing. This is why Abraham was such a joy to God's heart; he trusted Him. And this is why Sarah grieves Him. She did not believe that He would fulfill His promise. The LORD wants us to trust in His very great and precious promises because they are guaranteed by His perception and His power.

The LORD continues His comments as He directs us off of His perception and onto His power.

D. GOD'S POWER

Assurance – Genesis 18:14

> Is anything too difficult for the LORD? At the appointed time I will return to you, at this time next year, and Sarah will have a son.

Is anything too hard for the LORD? This is a rhetorical question that Abraham need not answer. Is anything too hard for the LORD? What is the answer from Scripture?

Jeremiah 32:17 tells us:

> Ah Lord GOD! Behold, You have made the heavens and the earth by Your great power and by Your outstretched arm! Nothing is too difficult for You.

Matthew 19:26 says:

> And looking at them Jesus said to them, "With men this is impossible, but with God all things are possible."

> Is anything to hard for the LORD? The rabbinic commentator Ha'amek Davar responds to the LORD's question with the statement:

> Nothing is beyond God; if He wished it, even a stone could conceive.[44]

Rabbi Malbim makes this comment:

> Since only HASHEM holds the key to conception ...
> age was never a factor because the laws of nature
> are neglected in the face of God's will.[45]

Nothing, absolutely nothing is too difficult for God. This is the lesson that Sarah had to learn. Is bringing a child from a dead womb too marvelous for the One who called all things into existence?[46] The LORD wants us to trust in His very great and precious promises because they are guaranteed by His perception and His power. At this point Sarah enters the conversation with a terse reply.[47]

Afraid - Genesis 18:15

> Sarah denied it however, saying, "I did not laugh";
> for she was afraid. And He said, "No, but you did
> laugh."

The writer quickly puts Sarah's reply aside as a lie. The Hebrew word means to deceive, to deny falsely[48], and to fly in the face of the facts.[49]

Why was Sarah willing to do this? Why was she willing to lie to God Himself? She was afraid. She was caught and exposed. When we are caught in our sin, our normal reaction is fear and denial. This reaction started with Adam and Eve in the Garden of Eden as recorded in Genesis 3:8-10.

The LORD gently rebukes her by repeating to her face the facts of the case. As the LORD rebuked Sarah for her unbelief, He removed that unbelief at the same time. As He solemnly reproved her, He proved to her that He knows all things, even her innermost thoughts. In this manner, true and full assurance of faith in God's word was created.[50] God broke down her unbelief and doubt through reproof. The results show that her unbelief was broken down because she did conceive and give birth to a son, a conception and birth that were framed in faith.[51]

Hebrews 11:11 reads as follows:

> By faith even Sarah herself received ability to conceive, even beyond the proper time of life, since she considered Him faithful who had promised.

This incident totally turned Sarah's attitude around. God worked a miracle in her heart before He worked a miracle in her body. The LORD wants us to trust in His very great and precious promises because they are guaranteed by His perception and His power.

E. APPLICATION

Let us now turn our attention from Abraham's success and Sarah's failure to our own reaction to the promises that God has given us. God has given us some promises that stagger the mind. Will we laugh in reverent, astounded, adoration and joy like Abraham, or will we laugh in derision like Sarah?

What are some of the very great and precious promises He has given to us? How about the promise of resurrection? That will boggle your mind.

In John 11:25-26 we read:

> Jesus said to her, "I am the resurrection and the life; he who believes in Me will live even if he dies, and everyone who lives and believes in Me will never die. Do you believe this?"

What an incredible, fantastic, unbelievable promise. Death is defeated! Do you believe it or is it simply a desperate dream that is too fantastic to be true?

What about some other promises? How about the Messianic Kingdom as recorded in Zechariah 14:9? We learn:

> And the LORD will be king over all the earth; in that
> day the LORD will be the only one, and His name
> the only one.

Do you rejoice in the amazing promise that *Yeshua* will someday rule this entire planet in righteousness and truth, or have the corrupt governments of this world made you incurably cynical?

Do you believe in a promise even more incredible than resurrection or the Messianic Kingdom? How about the promise that God loves you? 1 John 3:1 says:

> See how great a love the Father has bestowed
> upon us, that we should be called children of God;
> and such we are.

For some people this is the most unbelievable promise of all. Will you laugh with joy over this thought? Or will you doubt in your heart and say, "God can't possibly love me!"? Remember, God perceives that thought; He is eavesdropping on your mind, but He loves you anyway. Is God lying when He states that He loves you? Somehow, I don't think so.

How about another promise? Can you accept the promise that He will change you; He will remove all the dirty, painful stuff inside you and make you into a new person? We are told that He does this in 2 Corinthians 5:17:

> Therefore if any man is in Messiah, he is a new
> creature; the old things passed away; behold, new
> things have come.

Do you say, "Yes LORD, change me!" or do you say, "I am too dirty; I am too messed up; I am too rotten for God to be able to clean me up." Remember, He is able to do anything He wants.

What about the promise of salvation? We learn from reading John 5:24:

> Truly, truly, I say to you, he who hears My word,
> and believes Him who sent Me, has eternal life,
> and does not come into judgment, but has passed
> out of death into life.

Is your reaction to this promise, "Yes LORD, I receive you. I receive your gift and place my trust in you." Do you believe the Good News?

The Good News is found in 1 Corinthians 15:3-4. There it says:

> ...Christ died for our sins according to the
> Scriptures, and that He was buried, and that He
> was raised on the third day according to the
> Scriptures.

When you personally appropriate that simple message, it will change your eternal destiny. What a mind boggling promise! How can it possibly be true? It is true because that is the way God has chosen to do it, and God can do anything He wants to do.

If you have not already done so, will you personally accept the LORD into your life right now? What will be contained in your laugh...belief or disbelief, trust or distrust, faith or doubt? The choice is up to you. What will be contained in your laugh?

The LORD wants us to trust in His very great and precious promises because they are guaranteed by His perception and His power.

GENESIS 22:1-19
THE *AKEDAH*: THE BINDING OF ISAAC

A. PREFACE

Purpose Statement: Genesis

The general purpose of the Book of Genesis is to commence, preserve, and accurately communicate to men and their succeeding generations, information about God, man, and man's relationship to God. God begins by accurately informing us that He is the source of our physical origins. Genesis, therefore, reveals to us the origins of the universe, the earth, civilization, technology, and modern nations.

Next God uses the Book of Genesis to reveal to us our spiritual origins. God discloses our original spiritual state and close relationship to Himself. We are then shown the origin of sin which is the key overriding problem that severed man's relationship with God.

God does not simply inform us of this spiritual problem. He goes on to tell us of the beginning of the solution to the sin problem and its consequences of suffering and death. God begins to state His plan for returning His physical and spiritual creation to the condition experienced prior to corruption by sin.

His plan for the removal of this critical problem, sin, involves a specific nation. Therefore, another purpose of the Book of Genesis is to authoritatively record God's choice of individuals and their descendants, that is, the origin of the Jewish nation. Through His dealings with this nation, He begins to reveal the process He will use to work out His plan for mankind's redemption.

Context of the *Akedah*

God shows in the first 11 chapters of Genesis that mankind is inherently sinful and that the outward cleansing of the Noahic flood cannot rectify the inner condition of man's heart. Noah, the most righteous man on the earth at the time of the flood, still became the progenitor of a sin-loving race of people.

With the principle clearly seen that an inward problem cannot be solved by outward means, God now begins to focus in on the means He will use to cleanse man's internal sin nature. The means God chooses is the Principle of Faith. He will cleanse a man spiritually if that man voluntarily chooses to place his trust in God and thereby establish a personal relationship with God.

To show this He focuses on one man, Abraham. God uses Abraham as a model of living faith. By living faith we mean a trust in God that expresses itself through the daily life of the individual. Living faith goes beyond mere mental assent to facts about God. Rather, the decisions of a person's life are based on a trust in God's character. (James 2:14-24)

Prior to Genesis 22:1-19, we see Abraham growing in faith:

> The obedience of faith drew Abraham into a strange land; by the humility of faith he gave way to his nephew Lot; strong in faith he fought four kinds of the heathen with 318 men; firm in faith he rested on the word of promise, not withstanding all the opposition of reason and nature; bold in faith he entreated the preservation of Sodom under increasingly lowered conditions; joyful in faith, he received, named and circumcised the son of promise; with the loyalty of faith he submitted at the bidding of God to the will of Sarah and expelled Hagar and Ishmael; with the gratitude of faith he planted a tamarisk to the ever faithful God

in the place where Abimelech had sued for his friendship and accepted his presents, --now, his faith was to be put to the severest test to prove itself victorious . . .[54]

The *Akedah* – the binding of Isaac – is the high point of Abraham's faith, pointing out most clearly the distance that living faith is able to go if called upon to do so. God has now laid a strong foundation for His redemption program for mankind.

Continuing on in the Book of Genesis, we follow God's dealings in the life of Isaac. Isaac is a critical link, for Isaac's life of faith connects the father of the Jewish nation and the nation itself which had its origin in Jacob's twelve sons. It is through this nation that God will complete His plan of salvation, His kingdom program, and His covenant with Abraham.

B. INTRODUCTION

This section of scripture is one of the most meaningful portions of the Bible both for the Jewish community and the Christian community. For both communities this portion of Abraham's life stands as an impeccable example of commitment to and faith in God. Virtually every word of these 19 verses is full of deep significance and should be approached with care and respect.

C. EXPOSITION

God's Test – Genesis 22:1-2

Genesis 22:1a states,

> And it happened after these things,

This opening phrase takes us back to the preceding verse from chapter 21:34. "And Abraham sojourned in the land of the Philistines for many days." The word sojourned comes from the idea of being an alien rather than the word meaning to settle down in a permanent kind of manner. Abraham, the man of faith, was not allowing himself to become permanently attached to the things of this world, but kept himself in a state of readiness, alert to continue following God if the call came. However, while he "sojourned" rather than "settled," Jewish tradition states that he remained there in Beersheba for twenty-six years. This exact figure is, of course, conjecture on the Rabbi's part, but their opinion agrees with the thrust of Genesis 21:34 that even though Abraham was "sojourning," he remained in one place a long time ("many days"). The danger in this would lie in the fact that time and routine can be a great eroder of living faith. Time and routine causes us to redirect our attention to things, people, places, traditions, etc. rather than keeping focused on God. Although no time is expressly stated in the phrase "many days," there was perhaps time for Abraham to get lazy and relax in his faith commitment. Abraham had exhibited a life of faith to this point. What effect would time have upon him?

Another crucial aspect would include the fact that this test "occurred after Ishmael had been sent away when all hopes for the future and God's fulfillment of his promises were now centered only in Isaac."[55] Would Abraham be able to continue trusting God if it appeared that God would go contrary to His promises?

At this point, we come to Genesis 22:1 which says, "and it happened after these things" – "many days" – perhaps twenty-six years later when God calls to Abraham.

Genesis 22:1b:

> that God...

This phrase lets us know the source of Abraham's test, God Himself.

> The word did not come from his own heart, --was not a thought suggested by the sight of the human sacrifices of the Canaanites, that he would offer a

similar sacrifice to his God; nor did it originate with the tempter to evil. The word came from HaElohim, the personal, true God, who tried him by demanding the sacrifice of the only beloved son, as a proof and attestation of his faith.[56]

Genesis 22:1c

tested Abraham, and said to him, 'Abraham!'

The next phrase in the text reveals a reason for God's call, to test Abraham. This idea of testing should not be looked upon in a negative sense and should be differentiated from the idea of "tempt." "To tempt is to test, try, prove or solicit to do evil."[57] To tempt is not something that God does according to James 1:13. In contrast, to test someone is to prove his commitment to see how deep and strong it is. This God does do on a regular basis (James 1:1-12, 1 Peter 1:6-9). The principle of testing or examination by God being a beneficial experience is also well understood by the Jewish community. For example:

> *Ha Shem* examines (or tests) the righteous ones (Psa. 11:5) ... a potter does not examine defective vessels (i.e., demonstrate their strength to a potential buyer) because he cannot give them a single blow without breaking them. Where then does he examine? Only the sound vessels, for many blows will not break them.[58]

Abraham's test is interpreted positively by the Midrash which sees as the outcome of the test Abraham's exaltation by God.[59]

If however, we have determined that this testing was for good, why then did God require it? What was the result or results God expected to see? Two New Testament passages shed light upon God's reason for the Akedah. The first is Hebrews 11:17-18.

> By faith Abraham, when he was tested, offered up

> Isaac, and he who had received the promises was
> offering up his only begotten son; *it was he* to
> whom it was said, 'In Isaac your seed shall be
> called.'

From this passage we can see that God was testing Abraham's faith in God's character. God's referral to "seed" is a direct reference back to Genesis 12:1-3, the Abrahamic Covenant, in which God promised Abraham descendants (Gen. 12:2). Abraham was being asked to give up through sacrifice the only descendant of the promise. Isaac was unmarried at this time. How could he become a father of descendants if he died without a son? Abraham was facing the questions: Is God reliable? Is His character trustworthy? Can I trust Him to fulfill His unconditional promise to me?

The second passage that gives us insight into another reason for the test is James 2:20-22:

> But are you willing to recognize, you foolish fellow,
> that faith without works is useless? Was not
> Abraham our father justified by works when he
> offered up Isaac his son on the altar? *You see that
> faith was working with his works, and as a result
> of the works, faith was perfected.*" (Emphasis
> added)

The second reason for this test was that God was going to perfect and display Abraham's living faith through the *Akedah*. The *ArtScroll Tanach* commentary put it very succinctly:

> Anyone who has ever read scripture's account of
> the Akedah could not fail to recognize the
> awesome nature of the trial and the extraordinary
> extent of Abraham's faith. His belief in God has
> become indelibly inscribed in all who learned of
> his deed.[60]

Jewish tradition states that God addressing someone by his name is a sign of His love.[61] From this address we also see that Abraham had a close, personal relationship with God. This trial did not come from some aloof despotic sovereign bent on causing suffering, but from a God personally and intimately concerned with the maturing of His friend. When trials come our way, we too should remember that God is similarly working in our lives.

Genesis 22:1d continues,

> And he said, 'Here I am.'

Abraham's response to God is willing attention. The Jewish commentator, Rashi, explains:

> Such is the answer of the pious, the expression denoting both humility and readiness.[62]

Genesis 22:2a

> And He said, 'Please take'

With this phrase God begins to tell Abraham what He wants him to do. The expression in Hebrew is primarily and expression of entreaty.[63] It is a polite command as Rabbi Hertz explains:

> The Hebrew is peculiar: the imperative 'take' is followed by the Hebrew particle *nah* which means, 'I pray thee' – God is speaking to Abraham 'as friend to friend'.[64]

The language prevents us from interpreting this as a harshly worded, absolute command. God wanted Abraham to respond and "take" out of love, not terror.

Genesis 22:2b

> Take your son, your only son, whom you love, Isaac

Whom he was to take is now revealed to him. God's description of Isaac shows that God knew with crystal clarity Abraham's relationship to Isaac. "Your son" – he was Abraham's child, the child of promise, the child of the miraculous birth. "Your only son" – Isaac is described as "only" not because he was Abraham's only son in the physical sense since Abraham had already fathered Ishmael. Rather, he was the chosen son, the son of the promise. "Through Isaac your descendants shall be named" (Gen. 21:22). He was the son of the proper marriage, and "Abraham's name would be carried forth only through him."[65]

Genesis 22:2c

> and get yourself to the land of Moriah,

God now reveals to Abraham where he is to go. The significance of the location "the land of Moriah" is clearly stated in the Encyclopedia Judaica:

> The name Moriah... occurs elsewhere (II Chron. 3:1) as the name of the temple site. Hence, the Jewish tradition that the temple was built on the spot at which the *Akedah* took place.[66]

Genesis 22:2d

> and offer him there as a burnt offering on one of the mountains of which I will tell you.

Unless we have been faced with the loss of a child, we can never begin to understand the depth of emotion Abraham must have felt at this point. To who was he committed – to God or to himself? He is being asked to offer up all his hopes and dreams.

Abraham's Response – Genesis 22:3

Genesis 22:3a

> So Abraham rose early the next morning

Abraham swiftly obeyed. There is no mention of him taking counsel with flesh and blood. His obedience of faith was unwavering. Harav Michael Munk shares an insight:

> The implication of vayashken, awoke, is clear that Abraham actually slept that night. One can only marvel at his complete trust in God which allowed him to remain calm and serene despite the knowledge that he would set out the next morning to slaughter his beloved son.[67]

Genesis 22:3b

> and saddled his donkey, and took two of his young men with him and Isaac his son; and he split wood for the burnt offering,

This portion of verse 3 emphasizes Abraham's personal involvement in obeying God's command. As the head of the household, he could have had others do the menial tasks.[68] He, however, did not want to depend on others or the unforeseen. Obeying God was so important to him that he saw to it himself.

> It was a complete committal where everything was so carefully prepared that nothing could hinder the final fulfillment... we see Abraham's whole being: mind, emotions, actions united, concentrated entirely on full obedience.[69]

Genesis 22:3c

> and arose and went to the place which God had told him.

His obedience is precise and accurate, fulfilling entirely what God required.

Abraham's Arrival – Genesis 22:4-6

Genesis 22:4a

> On the third day

It is about a three day journey from Beersheba to Jerusalem, about 38 miles.[70] Abraham had three days to thoughtfully consider the matter he was undertaking, and because of his knowledge of God's power and trustworthiness, he came to this conclusion of faith: God would indeed fulfill His promises, and that He would even raise Isaac from the dead in order to do so. "By faith Abraham, when he was tested, offered up Isaac... He considered that God is able to raise men even from the dead..." (Heb. 11:17-19) Based upon this premise, Abraham continues to obey God and follow through with the sacrifice of Isaac.

Genesis 22:4b

> Abraham raised his eyes and saw the place from a
> distance.

The phrase in Hebrew always denotes "intentional looking up and around."[71] Abraham was deliberately searching for the place God was directing him to. He is still being diligent in his obedience and is not resentful or half-hearted.

In order to stress Abraham's and Isaac's spiritual commitment and sensitivity, the Midrash states the following story regarding this verse:

> Abraham said to Isaac, 'Do you see what I see?'
> He answered him, "I see a beautiful, praiseworthy
> mountain and a cloud attached to it.' (Abraham)
> said to his attendants, 'Do you see anything?'
> They said, 'We see nothing but deserts.' (Midrash
> Tanchuma, Vayeira 23).[72]

The point is well made. The spiritual man perceives with the eye of faith God at work in his life. The man lacking faith will see the scene from a totally different perspective. Abraham possessed the eye of faith pleasing to God, the kind of faith that does not degenerate into "good intentions" after three days but fulfills its commitment completely.

Genesis 22:5

> And Abraham said to his young men, 'Stay here
> with the donkey, and I and the lad will go yonder;
> and we will worship and return to you.'

Abraham's attitudes are shown very clearly to us in verse 5. First of all, this act would be done in private. Surely Abraham knew that his servants would not understand and perhaps even try to hinder the sacrifice of his son. He avoids any chance of being prevented from totally obeying God by this desire for privacy. Within the idea of privacy is the principle of separation. We need to separate ourselves from the distractions and things of the world that would hinder or prevent us from following God's will for our lives.

This set the tone for the most significant attitude that Abraham possessed, the attitude of worship as he performed this act. He was attributing worth to God by saying through this act that a relationship with God is worthwhile. This relationship is worth maintaining even if giving up what is nearest and dearest is required.

Finally, Abraham clearly announced his expectations. "We will... return to you." The rabbis declare that "at that moment the spirit of prophecy entered into him and he spoke more truly than he knew."[73]

Genesis 22:6

> And Abraham took the wood of the burnt offering

and laid it on Isaac his son, and he took in his
hand the fire and the knife. So the two of them
walked on together.

This was probably the hardest path a father ever walked with his
son. The phrase, later to be repeated in verse 8, "so the two of
them walked on together," is significant. It is significant because
apparently at this point Isaac is unaware of the true purpose for
the journey and the part he is to play. He is walking with his
father in harmony and unity, intent on facing whatever challenge
his father was facing together with him.

Isaac's Faith – Genesis 22:7-8

Genesis 22:7

And Isaac spoke to Abraham his father and said,
'My Father!' And he said, 'Here I am, my son.' And
he said, 'Behold, the fire and the wood, but where
is the lamb for the burnt offering?'

Isaac had been observing the special and unusual actions of his
father, and now, finally alone with him, wishes to know the
reasons for their journey.

Genesis 22:8a

And Abraham said, 'God will provide for Himself
the lamb for the burnt offering, my son.'

This is the correct answer, but it finds its origin in faith not in
sight. Abraham did not know how God would provide for his
need. This answer highlights a great principle of scripture. It is
our responsibility as believers to faithfully obey and leave the
answers to the things we cannot see with God.

Genesis 22:8b

So the two of them walked on together.

At this point the enigmatic phrase from verse 6 is repeated again. The phrase must have more significance than the repetition of the obvious fact that they continued walking. The significance lies in the fact that this phrase shows us Isaac's attitude of faith after his conversation with his father. The implication of verse 8 is that through this conversation with his father, Isaac now understood his role in the journey. Rashi comments on verses 6 and 8:

> (This is repeated to emphasize that) although Isaac now became aware that he was going to be slain, they still walked forward with a common purpose (and with no change of attitude).[74]

We rightfully focus on Abraham's faith in this section of scripture, but we must never miss the fact that Isaac was a man of commitment also, and his faith is a significant contribution to the story.

Obedience – Genesis 22:9-10

Genesis 22:9

> Then they came to the place of which God had told him; and Abraham built the altar there, and arranged the wood, and bound his son Isaac, and laid him on the altar on top of the wood.

This verse seems to be highlighting Abraham. It is true that we still see Abraham continuing to obey God completely. He personally builds the altar on the correct spot. He personally arranged the wood, binds his son, and lays him upon the altar. Abraham, at this moment, is the model of steadfastness, determination, and persistence. A little bit of Abraham is dying with each action, yet Abraham was orderly. "Abraham maintained his full presence of mind and thought and no act was impulsive."[75]

In contrast, however, we must understand that Isaac is present watching all this. It is one thing to prepare for the execution of another, but it is quite a different story to watch your own execution being deliberately, thoroughly and carefully prepared. Isaac does not voice objections, try to tearfully dissuade, forcefully resist, or simply run away. He too is a model of steadfastness and determination. Could Abraham at approximately 137 years of age force Isaac, who was about thirty-seven years old,[76] to be bound and laid on the altar of his own sacrifice? Of course not. Isaac who "lies without resistance like a lamb,"[77] submitted to being bound and prepared for death. "The glorious truth of this picture is that Isaac was a willing sacrifice."[78] Therefore, in verse 9 we see unparalleled obedience on Isaac's part.

Genesis 22:10

> And Abraham stretched out his hand, and took the knife to slay his son.

Now in verse 10 we can rightfully return our emphasis to Abraham's obedience.

> He raised the knife in his hand – at that point Abraham's surrender was proved complete. God knew that the hand that raised the knife would not hesitate to complete the action. From henceforth it was manifested to Abraham himself, to the world of every age, to angels and to demons, that Abraham loved God with a perfect love. Nothing, not even his only son, was allowed to stand between himself and God, who is Abraham's dearest treasure and rules supreme in his heart and life. From this time forth, Abraham would be completely and restfully conscious of his own complete identification with God who was his very life. At this moment all God's original purpose in His command of Genesis 22:2 had been

achieved. It had been necessary that Abraham's inner spirit should complete this total surrender: this was all God wanted, not the object itself. The test was completed.[79]

It now is incumbent upon God to intervene and prevent the death of Isaac.

God's Intervention – Genesis 22:11

Genesis 22:11a

> But the angel of the Lord called to him from heaven

It is significant that we first emphasize who called. It is the position of this writer that the angel of the Lord is none other than Jesus the Messiah, the second person of the Trinity, in a preincarnate appearance. The position regarding the significance of this angel will not be developed (please see *The Ryrie Study Bible*, page 30; *The New Scofield Reference Bible*, pages 289-290; and *Smith's Bible Dictionary*, page 36) other than to note that the Jewish community senses the significance of this being but is unable to recognize his full importance.

> How could Abraham obey an angel contradicting what he had heard expressly from God Himself? Furthermore, how could the angel have spoken in the first person?[80]

> The speaker may have been either the angel speaking in God's name, or God Himself.[81]

Questions and statements like these are easily resolved when we realize that the second person of the Trinity is speaking. The speaker is God Himself in a visible form.

Genesis 22:11b

> and said, 'Abraham, Abraham!'

As we noted earlier, when God calls a man by name, He is expressing His love for him. The rabbis, however, see even deeper significance in the repetition of a name. "His repeating a name indicated urgency."[82] This insight is validated by the Hebrew punctuation. "The two Abrahams are separated by a disjunctive mark (pause)."[83] There is a pause between the Abrahams indicating that Abraham was so intent on completing his act of obedience and worship that God had to literally yell at him a second time in order to break his concentration and gain his attention. Rabbi Hertz comments, "This exclamation shows the anxiety of the angel of the Lord to hold Abraham back at the very last moment."[84]

Genesis 22:11c

> And he said, 'Here I am.'

His attention redirected, Abraham responds by repeating the same statement of Genesis 22:1. In Hebrew, *Hineni* – that meaningful expression of willing attention. Abraham was willing to change direction at God's command. He was no blind fanatic. "His obedience was instant and unquestioning"[85] even if it meant a turn in the opposite direction. He was not mired down in his "program." Oh, that believers in this age might learn flexibility like Abraham's and not be rutted in our traditions. God has now successfully intervened and brought Abraham's test to its finish.

God's Satisfaction – Genesis 22:12

Genesis 22:12a

> And he said, 'Do not stretch out your hand against
> the lad, and do nothing to him;'

At this point God issues a command that Abraham take a new

direction. He is now to let Isaac live.

Genesis 22:12b

> for now I know that you fear God, since you have
> not withheld your son, your only son, from Me.

With this phrase God expresses His satisfaction with Abraham and Abraham's successful completion of the test of his faith.

This is a very interesting verse because in it there appears to be a contradiction in tenses. This apparent contradiction raises a question about the extent of God's knowledge. Is God all knowing or limited in knowledge? This question comes about because in the literal Hebrew, God is speaking in the past tense. He says, "I knew" or "have known that you fear God."[86] In contrast, the first word of the phrase "now" implies present tense. In other words, did God already know beforehand that Abraham feared Him or did He just come to that knowledge now? Kli Yakar resolves the question by explaining that the word "now" can have the connotation "behold."[87] We can, therefore, render the phrase "Behold, I knew that you fear God." This rendering solves the problem and brings God's omniscience clearly in view. As Barnhouse observes:

> The omniscient God knew from eternity what the
> outcome of this test would be, but now there is the
> full triumph of faith in the life of Abraham, and that
> would stand before all generations as an example
> of the utmost in faithful obedience.[88]

Rashi also very wisely interprets the verse:

> Now I can prove to Satan and all skeptics *what I
> have long since known* (emphasis added), for you
> have conclusively demonstrated that you are a
> God-fearing man.[89]

God's Provision – Genesis 22:13-14

Genesis 22:13a

> Then Abraham raised his eyes and looked, and
> behold, behind him a ram caught in the thicket by
> his horns.

A ram is now provided for the sacrifice. God is doing exactly what Abraham stated he would do in Genesis 22:8. He has met Abraham's need.

Genesis 22:13b

> And Abraham went and took the ram, and offered
> him up for a burnt offering *in the place of his son*
> (emphasis added).

One of the most important principles of the Biblical revelation is present in the final part of this verse. This statement deals with why the ram was sacrificed. The ram was a substitute for Isaac. The ram died in place of Isaac. This idea of substitution is developed throughout the scriptures until it finds its realization and culmination in the substitutionary sacrificial death of Jesus the Messiah (Matt. 20:28, Mark 10:45, 2 Cor. 5:11, 1 Peter 3:18). The Messiah dies in place of the sinner who trusts in Him.

Even though the Jewish community rejects the idea that Jesus is the fulfillment of the principle of substitution, they still very clearly see the principle in this story. Rashi says:

> The *Torah* specifies this to indicate that with each
> part of the sacrificial service which he performed
> on the ram, Abraham prayed to God that He
> accept that particular act *as if it were being done
> to his son* (emphasis added)... As though his
> blood were sprinkled; as though he were flayed;
> as though he were consumed and became
> ashes.[90]

And Bereishis Rabbah 56:14 pictures Abraham praying:

> (Abraham) said before Him, 'Master of the Universe, consider the blood of this ram *as if it were* (emphasis added) the blood of my son, Isaac; its parts *as if they were* (emphasis added) the parts of my son, Isaac.'[91]

Even with this kind of background from the Bible and rabbinic tradition, the Jewish community still cannot see the fulfillment of Isaiah 53:6 – "But the Lord has caused the iniquity of us all to fall on Him" – in the person of Jesus.

Genesis 22:14

> And Abraham called the name of that place The Lord Will Provide, as it is called to this day, 'In the mount of the Lord it will be provided.'

Abraham's response to God's provision is now explained to us. Abraham literally names the place "God will see," that is, God will see my needs and provide for them. The meaning of the name, however, is not limited to Abraham. God applies the thought to all believers in all time by validating the proverbial expression that follows Abraham actually naming the mountain. Regarding the proverb, Dr. Barnhouse observes:

> It should be translated, 'In the mount the Lord shall be seen.' This idea is that God will always intervene for His people in the hour of their need.[92]

And he wisely adds for those who view God as a quick panacea for their problems:

> He may not come at the time or in the way that our impatience may desire.[93]

God's Blessing – Genesis 22:15-18

Genesis 22:15-16a

> Then the angel of the Lord called to Abraham a
> second time from heaven, and said, 'By Myself I
> have sworn,' declares the Lord,

It is critical to note from this phrase who is pronouncing the
blessing. Hebrews 6:13 emphasizes this for us: "For when God
made the promise to Abraham, since He could swear by no one
greater, He swore by Himself." The significance of this is that the
promises that will now be given to Abraham will be unchangeable
and eternal. This significance is also realized by the rabbis:

> An irrevocable oath: Just as I am eternal, so is My
> oath eternal. (Radak)[94]

> Accordingly this was a solemn assurance of the
> ultimate redemption. (Ramban)[95]

Genesis 22:16b

> because you have done this thing, and have not
> withheld your son, your only son,

God now indicates why he is blessing Abraham. The word
"because" should not be viewed in the sense of earning, but
rather in the sense of "as a result of." Dr. Barnhouse observes:

> Nothing in man merits the grace of God. The
> promises of God are entirely free and result wholly
> from His sovereign grace. God frequently
> manifests His love toward us in consequence of
> something we alone have done.[96]

God delights in encouraging the life of faith, and He will reward
commitment to Him. Blessing inevitably follows obedience.

Genesis 22:17-18

> Indeed I will greatly bless you, and I will greatly
> multiply your descendants as the stars of the
> heavens, and as the sand which is on the
> seashore; and your descendants shall possess
> the gate of their enemies. And in your
> descendants all the nations of the earth shall be
> blessed, because you have obeyed My voice.

The blessing God bestows can be summed up succinctly in this way:

> The blessing was abundant. The blessing was in
> regard to the number of descendants. The
> blessing involved eventual victory over physical
> enemies. The blessing included spiritual blessings
> to all nations. Here the blessing is seen as a result
> of obedient faith.[97]

But there is more than a blessing occurring here. God is also confirming the Abrahamic Covenant of Genesis 12:1-3. He is repeating to Abraham two aspects of the Abrahamic Covenant and implying the third. God repeats the promises of a seed and world wide blessing. The land aspect is not expressly repeated, but by implication is included. The implication is that a nation of people need a geographical location to dwell in.

D. CONCLUSION – Genesis 22:19

Genesis 22:19

> So Abraham returned to his young men,

Just as Abraham had said he would, he returns to his servants, his faith vindicated, his knowledge of God increased, his relationship to God deepened. We can only imagine the joy and peace that filled his heart.

Genesis 22:19

and they arose and went together to Beersheba,
and Abraham lived at Beersheba.

Abraham now continues on with his life, but he is a different man. He had grown and matured from the experience, and he now had to pick up life where he had temporarily laid it aside. He could not remain on Mt. Moriah in the presence of God but had to put his faith into action again, this time in the normal, everyday decisions of his final years. Perhaps this aspect of his life, day to day faith, is as important as his binding of Isaac because he would now carry with him a new temptation, the temptation of pride.

The scriptures record no lapses of faith in the life of Abraham from this point on. He climbed his mountain, conquered the test, and continued with life unaffected by pride. He truly is the Father of the Faithful. We, as believers, must follow his example.

GENESIS 28:10-19
THE LADDER

Yeshua is the ladder, the mediator, and the house of God.

A. INTRODUCTION

The Abrahamic Covenant

Before we begin our study in Genesis 28:10-19, we need to review the Abrahamic Covenant found in Genesis 12:1-3 and have it firmly planted in our minds.

THE ABRAHAMIC COVENANT Eternal and Unconditional	**Land Promise (Israel)** ✿ To You ✿ To Your Descendents	**Land Covenant** Deut 29-30
	National Promise ✿ National Election ✿ Unique Relationship w/ Gentile Nations	**Davidic Covenant** 2 Sam 7:10-17 1 Chron 17:10-15 Ps 89:1-4, 19-37
	Spiritual Blessing Promise ✿ I will bless you. ✿ You will bless others	**New Covenant** Jer 31:31-34 Ezekiel 36:24-28

In the Abrahamic Covenant God makes three unconditional and eternal promises to Abraham *Avinu* -- to Abraham Our Father.

The three overarching promises of the Abrahamic Covenant consist of a land, a nation, and spiritual blessings. God progressively reveals more and more information about these three provisions as scripture unfolds.

The land aspect of the Abrahamic Covenant is presented in greater detail in the Land Covenant of Deuteronomy, chapters 29 and 30. The nation blessings are developed in the Davidic Covenant of 2 Samuel 7, 1 Chronicles 17, and Psalm 89. Finally, the spiritual blessings are explained and expanded in the New Covenant of Jeremiah 31:31-34 and Ezekiel 36:24-28.

This covenant was not made simply to Abraham alone but to Abraham and his offspring. As a result, God confirmed these blessings, first to Abraham's son Isaac, and then to Abraham's grandson Jacob. Isaac's confirmation came in Genesis 26 and the confirmation to Jacob comes in Genesis 28:10-19 which is the topic of this manuscript. Jacob will pass the Abrahamic Covenant on to his sons in Genesis chapter 49. From Genesis 49, the promises of the Abrahamic Covenant come down to Jewish people today in the 21st century.

As the curtain comes up on Genesis 28, it comes up on a family that has been shattered. Isaac's wife, Rebecca, has given birth to twin sons, each one very different from the other. Esau, the first born, is the physical man. He is a man of the open country, the skillful hunter, and he has little spiritual interests. He cares so little for the Abrahamic Covenant that he sells his birthright to Jacob for a single meal. The scripture states that he "despised his birthright" in Genesis 25:34.

Jacob, the younger twin, was a direct contrast to Esau. He was the spiritual man. He is described in scripture by the Hebrew word *tam*. *Tam* means to be sound, wholesome, one who is morally and ethically pure.[98] Jacob was a quiet sort of person who possessed integrity and who valued the spiritual side of life.

Now Jacob is not a perfect person. He has his flaws and shortcomings, as we will soon see, but at his core, deep in his soul, he loved God and he trusted God.

Favoritism had developed in Isaac's family due to the fact that these boys were so radically different in personality. Isaac loved the taste for wild game so he favored Esau while Rebecca favored her quiet son. This family, like many families, suffered from internal friction to begin with.

However, Isaac's family was totally destroyed when Isaac attempted to bless Esau with the Abrahamic Covenant. Rebecca and Jacob employed deception to gain what God would have given them anyway. This was a mistake, a lapse of trust in God. But they were successful in deceiving Isaac. Jacob was indeed blessed with the blessing rightfully due to him, but he and his mother shattered whatever harmony was in the family in the process.

Esau was enraged and planned to kill Jacob the moment his father died. Wisdom dictated that Jacob leave until his brothers hatred had abated. It was decided that Jacob should travel 450 miles to the north, to Haran, so he could find a wife from among his mother's relatives.

Isaac sent Jacob off with the words found in Genesis 28:4. He is speaking about God:

> May he give you and your descendants the blessing given to Abraham, so that you may take possession of the land where you now live as an alien, the land God gave to Abraham.

Isaac desires that the Abrahamic Covenant be confirmed as Jacob's possession. His desire will be granted in the upcoming verses.

Now we are ready to begin our study in Genesis 28. In verses 10 and 11, Jacob begins a remarkable journey.

B. THE LADDER

Remarkable Journey – Genesis 28:10-11

> Jacob left Beersheba and set out for Haran. When
> he reached a certain place, he stopped for the
> night because the sun had set. Taking one of the
> stones there, he put it under his head and lay
> down to sleep.

Jacob begins his remarkable journey in Beersheba where the
family was currently residing. Beersheba is located
approximately 43 miles to the south of Jerusalem. Jacob would
have traveled along the main route running along the top of the
Judean hills known as "the way to Ephrath" or "the central ridge
road." The modern Israeli road, Route 60, follows that exact
same path -- from Beersheba to Hebron to Bethlehem to
Jerusalem and then about 12 miles north of Jerusalem to Bethel.
As the sun sets, Jacob has been walking on the road for about
two or three days. He has covered a little over 50 miles on foot.
He makes camp near a town known as Luz and falls into an
exhausted sleep. He does not know it, but he has just made his
bed at a very significant spot.

The Hebrew text indicates that he "accidentally" picked this spot
at which to camp. He was not looking for this location, he just
happened upon it. However, we shall soon see that this is a
"divine happening."

Why is this campsite significant? The Hebrew indicates that he
has made his bed on the very same spot where his ancestor
Abraham erected an altar to the LORD.[99]

In Genesis 12, shortly after Abraham had entered the land of
promise, the LORD appeared to him in the region of Bethel.
Abraham worshipped the LORD at that very spot and built an
altar.

Shortly after that event, a famine came upon the Promised Land and Abraham left for food in Egypt. The experience in Egypt was harrowing when his beautiful wife, Sarai, was taken by the King of Egypt into his harem. God eventually rescued Abraham. Abraham then expressed his appreciation and trust by traveling back to Bethel and worshipping the LORD at that same altar.

Jacob is now, unknowingly, sleeping on that very spot. What an extraordinary "coincidence." His journey has indeed been a remarkable one so far.

As he sleeps, he experiences a remarkable dream as well.

Remarkable Dream – Genesis 28:12

> He had a dream in which he saw a stairway resting on the earth, with its top reaching to heaven, and the angels of God were ascending and descending on it.

On some occasions in scripture, dreams are used by God as vehicles of communication, vehicles of revelation.[100]

As Jacob sleeps, he sees a stairway or a ladder. (Ladder would be the preferred rendering.) He sees a ladder resting upon the earth with the top reaching up into heaven. Upon this ladder, angels from God are traveling up and down.

What is the meaning of this dream? Jacob's dream is unusual in that its interpretation, unlike other prophetic dreams recorded in scripture, is not given in the *Torah*.[101]

The rabbis offer at least eight various interpretations for us to consider. However, if we do not have an explanation of the dream in scripture, then unfortunately, each interpretation is purely speculation. Without the objective authority of scripture to go on, how do we know which interpretation is accurate? Are we lost here, out of luck, unable to understand the meaning of this dream? Fortunately, we do have an authoritative explanation of this dream elsewhere in scripture which we will get to in a few minutes.

So, in his dream, Jacob stands awestruck as he gazes at the ladder and at the angels and all their movement and activity. Suddenly Jacob's attention shifts off of the scene before him. He starts as he realizes someone is standing by his side.

C. REPEATED PROMISE

Nationally – Genesis 28:13-14

> There above it stood the LORD, and he said: 'I am the LORD, the God of your father Abraham and the God of Isaac. I will give you and your descendants the land on which you are lying. Your descendants will be like the dust of the earth, and you will spread out to the west and to the east, to the north and to the south. All peoples on earth will be blessed through you and your offspring.

The New International Version renders verse 13 with the idea that God stood above the ladder. However, the word translated "above" can also be rendered "beside" with equal validity depending upon the context. Here the translation can go one of four possible ways. God could be standing "above the ladder" or "beside the ladder." God could also be standing "above Jacob" or "beside Jacob."

We prefer the position that God is standing beside Jacob in that this is a very personal conversation between the two. However, God could just as easily be standing at the top of the ladder. It really makes no difference. You take your pick regarding which one you prefer. None of the four possibilities change the main point. The point is this: God has a message for Jacob.

God personally confirms that Jacob is the recipient of the Abrahamic Covenant.

Please note that all three elements of the Abrahamic Covenant are repeated. In verse 13 is says, "I will give you and your descendants the land on which you are lying." This is the land promise. The first part of verse 14 says, "Your descendants will be like the dust of the earth, and you will spread out to the west and to the east, to the north and to the south." That is the promise of a nation. The last part of verse 14 says, "All peoples on earth will be blessed through you and your offspring." That is the spiritual blessing element.

Now the rabbis have some pretty incredible statements to make regarding two of these provisions. In regard to verse 14, "Your descendants will be like the dust of the earth," we find this comment by Rabbi Ovadiah Sforno:

> Only after your offspring shall have become as degraded as the dust of the earth shall they spread out powerfully to the west, east, north, and south. For as the Sages have taught, God's future salvation will come only after Israel has experienced much degradation.[102] ...as it is written in Isaiah 59:20: 'The Redeemer will come to Zion, to those in Jacob who repent of their sins,' declares the LORD.

What Rabbi Sforno is saying is this. He sees this promise fulfilled by the institution of the Messianic Kingdom. However, he says, the Messianic Kingdom will not come until after Israel is trampled upon like the dust of the earth. Only after Israel is subjected to unprecedented degradation, only after Israel has been engulfed in suffering, will the redeemer, the Messiah, come to Zion. Rabbi Sforno is absolutely correct.

The unprecedented suffering that Israel will experience is known as the "Time of Jacob's Trouble" or as the "Tribulation." The Messiah, of course, is *Yeshua*, who Israel rejected when He came the first time offering the Messianic Kingdom. *Yeshua* said at that time that He would not return until Israel called Him back with the Messianic greeting of Psalm 118:26:

> Baruch haba b'shem Adonai -- Blessed is He who comes in the name of the LORD.

Only at the end of the Tribulation period will the Jewish people call out and beg *Yeshua* to return. That is when He will return to set up the Messianic Kingdom.

Rabbi Sforno's insight is totally consistent with the Messianic Jewish understanding of the prophetic future. It is truly an incredible insight for this rabbi to have.

In regard to the spiritual blessing aspect of the Abrahamic Covenant, Rabbi Shmuel ben Meir, the Rashbam, has an equally amazing comment to share. Rashbam feels that the secondary meaning of the word blessed is "to engraft." Accordingly, Rashbam renders the promise, "all the families of the earth will be grafted." That is: all the families of the earth will be engrafted into you; all the families of the earth shall join you. [103]

What does that sound like to you? It sounds like Rabbi Shaul, the Apostle Paul, in Romans 11:17-21. In that section of the *Brit Chadashah* (New Testament), the Jewish people are symbolized as a cultivated olive tree. Abraham is the root of that tree, Isaac and Jacob are the trunk, and the branches represent the people of Israel.

The gentiles are symbolized as a wild olive tree. Due to unbelief, some of the Jewish branches are broken off the cultivated tree. In contrast, when a gentile exercises faith and places his trust in *Yeshua*, then God cuts him off the wild olive tree and grafts him into the cultivated tree. When a gentile exercises faith in the God of Abraham, Isaac, and Jacob, through *Yeshua,* he or she is grafted in and shares the nourishing sap from the olive root.

Gentile believers do not become Jewish because a wild branch remains a wild branch; it does not change. However, they are grafted into the place of spiritual blessing exactly as Rashbam understands the spiritual blessing promise of the Abrahamic Covenant. This is, indeed, how all the families of the earth will be blessed through the Abrahamic Covenant. Through Messiah *Yeshua,* they are grafted into the place of spiritual blessing.[104]

And do you know what Rabbi Shaul does immediately after talking about the Gentiles being grafted into the place of blessing? He quotes Isaiah 59:20. He quotes the very same verse that Rabbi Sforno quoted:

> 'The Redeemer will come to Zion, to those in Jacob who repent of their sins,' declares the LORD.

Rabbi Shaul likewise connects the spiritual blessing aspect of the Abrahamic Covenant with the end of the age and the institution of the Messianic Kingdom. Rashbam has an amazing and accurate insight into the blessing promise of the Abrahamic Covenant. This promise will reach its climax when the Kingdom begins.

At this point, God has made some general overarching promises to Jacob. Now, God changes His emphasis. Now, God gets very personal with Jacob.

Personally – Genesis 28:15

> I am with you and will watch over you wherever you go, and I will bring you back to this land. I will not leave you until I have done what I have promised you.

Here *HaShem* personally encourages Jacob. First, He encourages Jacob with the promise of His presence. Jacob need not fear the future. Jacob need not fear the past. God will personally be with him and care for him. Secondly, God solemnly states that He is a promise keeper. He will fulfill the Abrahamic Covenant. He will do for Jacob everything He said He would do. The place of God was by his side, guiding him through life and leading him to future greatness. [105]

Jacob's reverent response is revealed in verses 16-17.

Reverent Response – Genesis 28:16-17

> When Jacob awoke from his sleep, he thought, 'Surely the LORD is in this place, and I was not aware of it.' He was afraid and said, 'How awesome is this place! This is none other than the house of God; this is the gate of heaven.'

Jacob is awestruck by the revelation he had received. He might have felt that he was all alone, exiled from his family, going who knows where, but now he knows that God is with him. Now he knows without a shadow of a doubt that God loves him and cares for him. There may be estrangement -- alienation between Jacob and his family, but there is not separation between him and God.

In verses 18 and 19 he sets up a monument to a miracle -- he creates a reminder so that he will never forget what has happened.

Reminder – Genesis 28:18-19

> Early the next morning Jacob took the stone he had placed under his head and set it up as a pillar and poured oil on top of it. He called that place Bethel, though the city used to be called Luz.

Jacob waits until the morning light and sets up a simple monument to his experience. He sets his stone pillow upright as a small pillar and then anoints it with oil as a symbol of consecration. For Jacob, this piece of ground will always have special significance. He renames the area Bethel -- house of God -- as an additional reminder of the astounding vision and message he received.

At this point in our text the message from God to Jacob is pretty clear. However, the meaning of the ladder has still not yet been explained. That part of the dream has not been made clear to the reader. The explanation of the ladder will not be revealed for another 1,900 years. The explanation of Jacob's dream will be revealed by *Yeshua* himself in John 1:45-51.

In that section of the *Brit Chadashah*, *Yeshua* gathers his disciples. He begins with John and Andrew. Andrew then gets his brother, Simon Peter. The next day *Yeshua* adds Philip to His growing band of disciples. Philip, in turn, goes after Nathaniel -- and that is where we pick up the story in John 1:45.

D. MESSIANIC SIGNIFICANCE - John 1:45-51

John 1:45-49 says:

> Philip found Nathaniel and told him, 'We have found the one Moses wrote about in the Law, and about whom the prophets also wrote—Jesus of Nazareth, the son of Joseph.' 'Nazareth! Can anything good come form there?' Nathaniel asked. 'Come and see,' said Philip. When Jesus saw Nathaniel approaching, he said of him, 'Here is a true Israelite, in whom there is nothing false.' 'How do you know me?' Nathaniel asked. Jesus answered, 'I saw you while you were still under the fig tree before Philip called you.' Then Nathaniel declared, 'Rabbi, you are the Son of God, you are the King of Israel.'

Does this conversation strike you as rather odd? Think about it. Would you proclaim a perfect stranger to be your King just because he happened to see you under a fig tree? What in the world is going on in Nathaniel's mind?

To understand the conversation, we have to take a close look at the context as well as the Jewish background of the period.

If you look at verse 47, you will notice that *Yeshua* called Nathaniel "an Israelite." Then, after calling him by the term "Israel," he says that there is nothing false in Nathaniel.

Yeshua is intending to draw a specific contrast here. The first person ever to be called Israel was Jacob. Jacob basically was an upright man -- he was "*tam.*" His life was not characterized by falsehood. However, there was one serious incident of falsehood that did impact Jacob's life considerably. He was guilty of one act of falsehood when he deceived his father. Because of that one act of falsehood, we find Jacob estranged from his family and traveling to Haran.

In contrast to the first Israelite, this Israelite, this descendant of Jacob, is characterized by an absence of any falsehood. We can see that in the conversations that we just read.

Nathaniel could be described by the phrase "what you see is what you get." He speaks out what he is thinking; he doesn't hide anything. He may not have a lot of tact, but he has a transparent personality. He is not a hypocrite, and he is not a deceiver.

Then in verse 48, *Yeshua* says that He saw Nathaniel "under the fig tree." *Yeshua* is not merely talking about seeing Nathaniel sitting in the shade. That was not unusual. Many people saw Nathaniel sitting in the shade. Nothing could be more ordinary and commonplace.

The question we have to ask is, "What was Nathaniel *doing* under the fig tree?"

In those days, it was impossible for everyone to possess their own personal copy of the scriptures. As a result, the Jewish people spent a lot of their time memorizing scripture. When you went to the Synagogue school, the reader would recite the passage, and you would memorize it by repetition. Once you had that passage memorized, usually in chunks of about a chapter or so, then you would meditate upon what you memorized to make sure that it stuck.

The rabbis taught that the best place to meditate on the scriptures was -- guess where -- under a fig tree.[106]

The fig tree is significant in the thinking of the rabbis because it is a symbol of peace and prosperity, safety and leisure.[107]

For example, 1 Kings 4:25 says:

> During Solomon's lifetime Judah and Israel, from Dan to Beersheba, lived in safety, each man under his own vine and fig tree.

This symbol of peace and prosperity, safety and leisure is likewise associated with the Messianic kingdom.

In the context of the Messiah and the Messianic Kingdom, Micah and Zechariah have these words to share with us. Micah 4:4 says:

> Every man will sit under his own vine and under his own fig tree, and no one will make them afraid, for the LORD Almighty has spoken.

Zechariah 3:10 reads:

> 'In that day each of you will invite his neighbor to sit under his vine and fig tree,' declares the LORD Almighty.

With this kind of a biblical background, the fig tree took on important significance. The *Midrash* states that one of the more famous rabbis, Rabbi Akiva, would hold his discipleship classes under a fig tree because he felt that under a fig tree is the best place to meditate on scripture.

In view of this background, we can conclude that Nathaniel was meditating on scripture under that fig tree.

When *Yeshua* spoke of him being an Israelite without falsehood, he realized that *Yeshua* knew the exact section of scripture that he was meditating on. *Yeshua* could read his mind.[108] The ability of *Yeshua* to read minds is a characteristic of the Messiah.

This understanding of the supernatural power of the Messianic person is based on Isaiah 11:3 which reads:

> He will not judge by what he sees with his eyes, or
> decide by what he hears with his ears...

On the basis of Isaiah 11:3, the rabbis taught that the Messiah would be able to make righteous judgments by means other than the natural senses -- the eyes or the ears.

To quote Rabbi Ibn Ezra on Isaiah 11:3:

> He will not be guided by the superficial impressions of the
> senses.[109]

It has suddenly become very clear to Nathaniel that this man is operating beyond the realm of the five senses. Since he has been taught all his life that this is a Messianic characteristic, he jumps to the correct conclusion, "You are the Messianic King."

Let us continue on in John 1 with verses 50 and 51:

> Jesus said, 'You believe because I told you I saw
> you under the fig tree. You shall see greater
> things than that.' He then added, 'I tell you the
> truth, you shall see heaven open, and the angels
> of God ascending and descending on the Son of
> Man.'

Yeshua continues the conversation by referring to our *Torah* portion -- Genesis 28. The reason *Yeshua* mentions this is because this was the very passage of scripture that Nathaniel was meditating on as he sat under that fig tree.[110] *Yeshua* read Nathaniel's mind and this shocked Nathaniel into recognizing that *Yeshua* was the Messianic King.

But *Yeshua* does not stop there. *Yeshua* now goes on to interpret the dream that Jacob had. He tells Nathaniel, "You have come to faith because of a little miracle – I have read your mind. You are going to witness greater things than the Messiah reading your mind. You are going to witness something as great as your ancestor Jacob saw."

Now He gives the interpretation that we have waited 1,900 years to hear.

The implication would be that Nathaniel was pondering or meditating on the meaning of the ladder as he sat under that fig tree. *Yeshua* gives Nathaniel the answer to his question, the answer to his contemplation. He tells Nathaniel that he will see the "angels ascending and descending upon the Son of Man."

This title, Son of Man, was a technical expression in the first century for "the Messiah."[111] It is based on Daniel 7:13.[112]

In other words, *Yeshua* tells Nathaniel that the Son of Man, the Messiah, that He Himself, *Yeshua*, is the ladder. In the dream, the ladder was the link between heaven and earth. Likewise, *Yeshua* is God's link with earth (cf. Dan. 7:13; Matt. 26:64).[113] *Yeshua* is the divine communication from heaven to earth.[114] *Yeshua* is the ladder because He is the way to the Father.[115]

Yeshua said of Himself in John 14:6:

> I am the way and the truth and the life. No one comes to the Father except through me.

There is only one ladder that gives man access to heaven, and that ladder is the holy, righteous, and divine Messiah.

Yeshua is also the mediator between God and man. The function of a mediator is to intervene between two parties in order to promote relations between them which the parties themselves are not able to effect. The situation requiring a mediator is often one of estrangement and alienation, and the mediator effects reconciliation.[116]

This is exactly what *Yeshua* came to do. He came to reconcile us to God because we are alienated from Him because of our sins.

Yeshua is also the mediator of the New Covenant (Heb. 9:15; 12:24). It is though Him, and Him alone, that intimate fellowship with God is possible.

Jacob called the place where this happened "Bethel" because he felt that it was the "house of God" or "the gate of heaven." That is not quite right. There is a gate of heaven, but it is not found at any particular location on earth. The true gate of heaven is *Yeshua,* and access to Him is available to every man or woman on earth.

You open the gate of heaven by exercising faith, by exercising trust in *Yeshua.* You see, *Yeshua* is not only the ladder. *Yeshua* is also Bethel, as well. *Yeshua* is the ultimate and perfect "house of God."

So now the mystery of Jacob's dream, the mystery of the ladder, has been solved. The Messiah would be the ladder, the mediator, the gate between man and God. He would come in order to overcome the estrangement and alienation caused by sins such as falsehood and deception. Those sins had shattered Jacob's family. However, in the future, God would but the pieces of this shattered family back together again.

E. APPLICATION

The context in which Jacob's ladder appears is very significant. When Jacob's ladder appears in *Tenach,* it is in the context of a shattered family and healing is promised. When Jacob's ladder appears in the *Brit Chadashah,* it is in the context of a family being gathered together. *Yeshua* is gathering His family. He is beginning with these few disciples, and the process is still going on around the world. In *Yeshua,* spiritual and physical and social healing all have their source.

Are you in need of spiritual, physical or family healing? Your source of that healing is *Yeshua,* the ladder, the mediator, the house of God. If you want this healing, you have to come to Him in faith. You have to trust Him so that you can receive the healing that He wants to give you

The Emblem of Jerusalem

GENESIS 49:1-12
JUDAH AND MESSIAH

Our personal character growth will determine our
rewards in this world and in the world to come

A. INTRODUCTION

We now come to an extremely significant Messianic prophecy.
However, before we begin to examine this text, we need to briefly
discuss the context in which the prophecy is found.

The background actually begins with Abraham *Avinu* or
Abraham, Our Father. God called him out of Ur of the Chaldees
and told him to start a new life in the Promised Land. In addition,
God entered into a covenant with Abraham and guaranteed that
a nation would spring from him. Abraham's family then began to
increase, slowly at first, beginning with Abraham's son, Isaac,
and then Isaac's son, Jacob.

In Genesis 49, Jacob's family has now increased to 12 sons, as
well as numerous grandchildren and dependents. They have
moved from Canaan to Egypt to sojourn there under the
protection of the wise and powerful son, Joseph.

As our chapter opens, the aged patriarch, Jacob, lays dying upon
his bed. In accordance with tradition, he is about to pass on the
Abrahamic Covenant to all 12 of his sons. As he does this, he
foretells the future of the nation that will develop from these 12
men. Then, most importantly, he predicts the coming of the
Messiah King.

As Jacob pronounces his revelation from God, we will learn

something. We will see that our personal character growth determines our rewards in this world and in the world to come.

B. JUDAH AND MESSIAH

Assembling the Tribes - Genesis 49:1-2

> Then Jacob called for his sons and said: "Gather around so I can tell you what will happen to you in days to come. Assemble and listen, sons of Jacob; listen to your father Israel."

Jacob deliberately gathers his sons about his death bed for the purpose of passing on a message to them.

We are clearly told in verse 1 that Jacob will be speaking about those things that will happen in "the last days" or as the New American Standard Bible (NASB) states, "in the days to come." This term "the last days" or "in the days to come" projects Jacob's comments into the far distant future.

In most cases, depending on the context, the phrase "in the last days" refers to the end of the age that we are living in right now and will culminate with the institution of the Messianic Kingdom. This position is likewise the position of almost all the ancient Jewish commentators as well.

For example, Nachmanides, Sforno, and Rambam all concur that Jacob is peering down the conduit of time toward the Messianic era. He is looking toward the institution of the Messianic Kingdom.

In other words, God is revealing to Jacob the future history of his descendants. The sons of Jacob assemble around his death bed as the representatives of the 12 tribes. They represent the entire Jewish people because the revelation goes far beyond these dozen men. The revelation summarizes the characteristics of the entire Jewish people from Jacob's day until the Messianic Kingdom.

Jacob's opening comments are negative. Three of his sons, three tribes, will be disqualified from leadership over Israel. They will be disqualified because of serious character flaws they could not rise above.

Jacob's attention is first directed to his oldest son Reuben in verses 3-4.

C. DISQUALIFIED FOR LEADERSHIP

Reuben for Lack of Self Control[117] - Genesis 49:3-4

> Reuben, you are my firstborn, my might, the first sign of my strength, excelling in honor, excelling in power. Turbulent as the waters, you will no longer excel, for you went up onto your father's bed, onto my couch and defiled it.

Reuben was the biological firstborn, and as such should have been Jacob's spiritual heir. According to natural right, he was entitled to the first rank among his brothers, to the leadership of the tribes, and to a double share of the inheritance. Reuben has forfeited, Reuben has lost these privileges.

The question naturally arises, "What caused this loss, this forfeiture?"

Jacob answers that question in verse 4 by describing Reuben's moral character. He compares Reuben to an uncontrolled, destructive flood pounding through a dry wadi in the Holy Land. Like a churning, gushing torrent of waters, he possessed no moral self control. That lack of self discipline overflowed its banks one time too many in an incident of moral indiscretion that humiliated his father. The explanation is brief and to the point, "for you went up onto your father's bed, onto my couch and defiled it." Jacob's comment is a reference to Genesis 35:22 where Reuben slept with Jacob's concubine, Bilhah. Reuben violated the honor of his father and so lost the leadership in

Israel. As a result, his tribe attained to no position of influence in the nation. Reuben had birth, dignity, and opportunity, but he had no strength of character.

To quote Rabbi Hertz from the Hertz Pentateuch:

> Here Scripture stresses the idea that moral character is a more important factor than hereditary right.[118]

Our personal character growth will determine our rewards in this world. If we are immoral, like Rueben, we will suffer the consequences of immorality as well. Jacob's remarks to Reuben are complete.

Jacob now moves on to the next two sons in seniority, Simeon and Levi in verses 5-7.

Simeon and Levi for Cruelty[119] - Genesis 49:5-7

> Simeon and Levi are brothers—their swords are weapons of violence. Let me not enter their council, let me not join their assembly, for they have killed men in their anger and hamstrung oxen as they pleased. Cursed be their anger, so fierce, and the fury, so cruel! I will scatter them in Jacob and disperse them in Israel.

Reuben was Jacob's firstborn, Simeon was his second born, and Levi his third born. Jacob explains to Simeon and Levi that the dignities which Reuben had forfeited should have been theirs as the next in line. However, they too were unworthy of them because of their cruelty.

Simeon and Levi are grouped together because they were the instigators of the bloodshed against the city of Shechem in Genesis 34:25. They were not simply biological brothers. They were also brothers in thought and in action, in counsel and deed, in violence and in cruelty. Jacob protested vehemently against the two sons and their attack on the defenseless city. Here he gives his final verdict on their action. The two tribes would loose their portion of territory in the land. Simeon eventually became the weakest of all the tribes. Simeon received no separate assignment of territory as an inheritance. He merely received a number of cities within the territory of Judah. Simeon was eventually absorbed into Judah. Levi also received no separate inheritance in the land. Levi received merely a number of cities to dwell in scattered throughout the possessions of his brothers.

However, the scattering of Levi was changed into a blessing because they received the privilege of the priesthood. In Exodus 32:29, the Levites stood committed to the LORD when the rest of the nation worshipped the golden calf. Because of that commitment, they were set apart by the LORD for special use. Eventually they became the priestly tribe. Scattered as priests throughout the country, they were responsible to teach the nation the Holy Scriptures.

Before we leave this section, please notice a principle that the Jewish commentator Rashi brings out. Rashi observes Jacob's curse in verse 7. He states, "He did not curse *them*, but their anger."[120] We often make this statement: "God hates the sin but loves the sinner." As Rashi notes, this is an example of that principle in operation.

The Talmud, Berachos 10A states it this way:

> The righteous pray for the destruction of sin, but not of sinners. Let the sinners repent so that they will survive while their sins will no longer exist.

That is exactly what we want, isn't it? That is exactly why we proclaim the Gospel. We want sinners to repent and be saved from the wrath of God.

Simeon and Levi suffered discipline for their failings, but they were not excluded from the nation of Israel. God loved them, but not their sin. They were merely put into the background because of their sins, but they did not loose out of their part in the Abrahamic Covenant.

The same is true for us. No genuine believer will ever lose the gift of eternal life that God has given him through trusting *Yeshua* (Jesus). However, we may be put into the background because of our sins. Our personal character growth will determine our rewards in this world. If we are cruel and violent, like Simeon and Levi, we will reap the consequences of cruelty and violence as well.

We now move on to Jacob's fourth son, Judah, in verses 8-9.

D. QUALIFIED FOR LEADERSHIP

Judah – Genesis 49:8-9

> Judah, your brothers will praise you; your hand will be on the neck of your enemies; your father's sons will bow down to you. You are a lion's cub, O Judah; you return from the pray, my son. Like a lion he crouches and lies down, like a lioness— who dares to rouse him?

Judah, the fourth son, was the first to receive a rich and unmixed blessing, the blessing of supremacy and power. Judah's name means "praised."[121] Jacob foretold a future for the tribe of Judah that pictured him as the preeminent son—the prominent tribe. This is a promise of leadership, of victory, and of tribal stability.[122] In the future history of the tribe, Judah would become all that his name implied. The tribe would be praised. In verse 8, Judah is also described as a victorious warrior. He returns home from battle to be greeted by shouts of praise from his brothers. The idea of the victorious warrior is extended and enlarged through the image of Judah as a lion in verse 9.

There is a progression, a process of development apparent in the lion metaphor. Judah is pictured as a playful, frolicking, fighting, and vigorous young one who develops into a powerful and awesome animal.[123] Growth and development are part of the picture here. A rhetorical question brings the image to a close, "who dares to rouse him?" No answer is needed, it is too obvious. You do not mess with a mature, healthy lion. Only the most foolish of fools would dare disturb such a dangerous beast.

Judah, as a person, was not a perfect person; he had his flaws. For example: He was partner to selling his brother Joseph into slavery in Genesis 37. He wronged his daughter-in-law Tamar in Genesis 38.

However, Judah possessed a basic nobility of character that grew in strength as the years passed. This growth in personal character and moral integrity enabled him to overcome the flaws in his personality. He overcame his deficiencies unlike his three older brothers. For example: He offered himself to Joseph as a guarantee of Benjamin's safety in Genesis 43. He followed through on that pledge in Genesis 44 by offering to become a slave in Benjamin's place.

For this growth, for this direction of his life, he is commended. This basic nobility of character will mark his tribe for years to come. They will grow to become the single most dominant tribe in the centuries to follow.

Our personal character growth will determine our rewards in this world. If we mature in character, like Judah, we will reap the rewards of character as well.

Now Jacob continues his remarks, and as he does, he begins to speak about another of his sons. This son is not one of the 12 gathered about his bed. This is a descendent that will come from the tribe of Judah some 1,700 years in the future.

In verses 10-12, Jacob now begins to describe the Messiah and the Messianic Kingdom.

E. MESSIAH AND THE MESSIANIC KINGDOM

Timing – Genesis 49:10

> The scepter will not depart from Judah, nor the
> ruler's staff from between his feet until he comes
> to whom it belongs and the obedience of the
> nations is his.

This verse is an extremely significant Messianic verse.

Quoting from the Artscroll *Tenach* commentary, an orthodox
Jewish commentary, Rabbi Zlotowitz, one of the editors, makes
this remark:

> The general consensus [with few exceptions] of
> rabbinic interpretation is that this phrase refers to
> the coming of the Messiah. This passage
> accordingly constitutes the primary *Torah* source
> for the belief that the Messiah will come.[124]

> ... the overwhelming consensus of Rabbinic
> Commentary interprets this verse to allude to the
> Messiah.[125]

According to Rabbi Zlotowitz, this verse is the foundation verse.
This is the bedrock verse from which our understanding of the
Messiah's coming will grow. At least 13 prominent rabbinic
commentators agree that this is a Messianic verse, and to get 13
Jewish people to agree on anything is a miracle in itself.

Rashi says that the verse refers to the Messiah.[126] Targum
Onkelos renders the verse as referring to the Messiah.[127]
Nachmanides agrees,[128] as does Rabbi Ashtruc in the
commentary Midrashei *Torah*,[129] and Gur Aryeh,[130] and Rabbi
Sforno,[131] and Midrash Tanchuma,[132] the Jerusalem Targum,
Targum Pseudo-Jonathan, Yalkut, the Talmud,[134] and Midrash
Rabbah.[135]

It is no wonder that Rabbi Zlotowitz states:

> ...the overwhelming consensus of Rabbinic Commentary interprets this verse to allude to the Messiah.[136]

Let us examine such an important verse of Sacred Scripture. We begin with the scepter in verse 10.

The scepter first began as the shepherd's staff. Israel's rulers are also considered to be the shepherd of their people. This may be one of the reasons why God chose David to be Israel's king. David had been a shepherd. As such, he gained a proper understanding of the leadership role. This is also why *Yeshua* referred to himself as the "good shepherd."

The scepter is also an emblem of kingship[137] and a symbol of regal command.[138] In the hand of the ruler, it became a symbol of his power.[139] The king held the scepter in his hand while speaking in public assemblies. When he sat upon his throne, he rested it between his feet and inclined it toward himself.

The concept has carried over into our day, into the body of the Messiah. The leaders of a local congregation are considered to be under-shepherds of the "good shepherd."

At this point, we come to a phrase in verse 10 that has caused the spilling of untold gallons of ink on paper. The phrase is the statement rendered by the NASB, "until Shiloh comes." Five different positions have been generated by this difficult phrase, each with its own supporters. We will not develop all five positions. Suffice it to say, we will look at the position that has the most textual support and that fits the context.

The exact wording of the statement varies between translations. Many English versions render the statement something like this: "The scepter shall not depart from Judah, nor the ruler's staff from between his feet, *until Shiloh comes...*" This approach makes "Shiloh" a title for the Messiah. As such, Genesis 49:10 became the source for the rabbinic name of the Messiah.[140]

For example, Sanhedrin 98a says:

> What is the name of the Messiah? They of the school of Rav Shila said, "His name is Shiloh."

Unfortunately, using the word "Shiloh" as if it were a proper name for Messiah obscures the meaning of the phrase.[141]

This word "Shiloh" should be taken as a possessive pronoun, not a proper name. This is how the Septuagint translates the verse, as does the Syriac version. This reading is further supported by a comparison with Ezekiel 21:27.[142] In Ezekiel 21:27, a similar phrase and construction is used.

Therefore, the best translation has been done by the New International Version (NIV):

> The scepter will not depart from Judah, nor the ruler's staff from between his feet, until he comes to whom it belongs...

The point is that Judah's identity and right to rule cannot be lost until someone comes who has full rights to the scepter. Judah's superiority cannot be lost until someone comes who has full claim to the right to rule. Those who reign from the house of Judah will do so in anticipation of the one to whom the kingship truly belongs.

Now we need to turn our attention to that little time indicator "until." The prophecy pivots around the word "until."

The scepter (the ruler's staff and Judah's dominance) will not depart "until" after the Messiah appears. This is the real key and significance of the verse. The Messiah will have to come before the tribe of Judah loses its prominence and identity. This establishes a clear time period for the prophecy. The timing of the Messiah's appearance is the most important point.

When did the tribe of Judah lose its prominence and identity? The records of tribal identities were kept and maintained in the Temple. All of these records were lost with the destruction of the temple in 70AD. Within a few generations all the tribes of Israel, with the exception of Levi, had lost their identity. Since the tribe of Judah lost its pre-eminence and identity in 70AD, it can clearly be seen that the Messiah must have come sometime before 70AD. It is not possible for the Messiah to come after 70AD.[143]

There is a fascinating comment found in the Rabbinic writings that corresponds with this.

> Rabbi Rachmon says: "when the members of the Sanhedrim found themselves deprived of their right over life and death, a general consternation took possession of them; they covered their heads with ashes and their bodies with sackcloth, exclaiming: 'Woe unto us, for the scepter has departed from Judah, and the Messiah has not come?'"[144]

The Sanhedrin was wrong. In 30AD, the Messiah had come, exactly as Genesis 49:10 had predicted. The point is that the ancient Jewish interpretation recognized unmistakably that a time frame for the Messiah's coming is clearly laid out in Genesis 49:10. However, the Jewish people refused to heed the information. The scepter was taken away from Judah at that precise moment so that the Romans would crucify *Yeshua*. Psalm 22 and *Yeshua* both predicted that he would be crucified. Therefore, the scepter was removed from Judah at that precise moment to fulfill God's word.

Verse 10, to this point, brings us to the first coming of the Messiah. This passage can only be speaking of one person. There is only one person in history that lived before 70AD, who fulfills the requirements of the passage, and who claimed to be the Messiah. That person is Yeshua. Yeshua's earthly career began with His birth in 6 or 7AD and terminated with His ascension in 30AD.

In Luke 3, we have a record of His genealogy, His tribal identity. We know what tribe and family Yeshua came from. Yeshua is a descendent of Judah as well as a descendent of the royal family of David. In Luke 1, Yeshua is stated to be the final king of Judah's royal supremacy.

The angel Gabriel announced the birth of the Messiah to Mary. He makes this statement in Luke 1:31-33:

> You will be with child and give birth to a son, and you are to give him the name Yeshua. He will be great and will be called the Son of the Most High. The Lord God will give him the throne of his father David, and he will reign over the house of Jacob forever; his kingdom will never end.

Judah's prominence reaches its greatest glory with the coming of Yeshua. However, we the Jewish people rejected Yeshua as our Messiah/King when He came the first time. Yeshua went back to His heavenly throne until the time when the Jewish people shall call on Him to return. It is at that time, sometime in the future, He will return to destroy His enemies and institute the Messianic Kingdom. Because of this fact of history, we have a time gap between what we have seen so far and the last phrase of the verse.

Please refer to the diagram on the following page. This is how the timing of each phrase breaks down.

"The scepter will not depart from Judah, nor the ruler's staff from between his feet," refers to the time period from 1,700BC to 6-7BC.

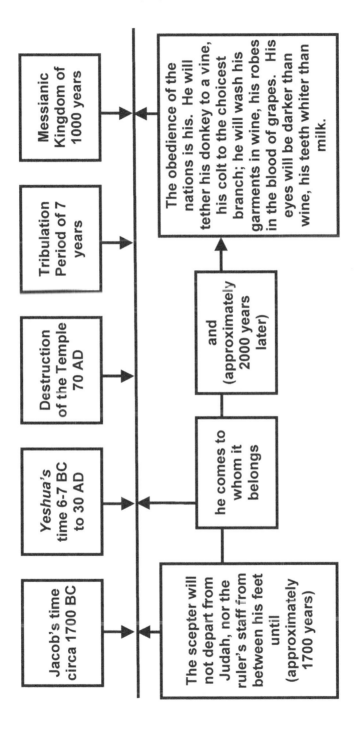

The word "until" brings us to *Yeshua's* first coming, 6 or 7BC to 30AD.

Then a time gap exists between that phrase and the final phrase of the verse. That time gap is covered by that little connective word "and." That little word "and" covers the time from 30AD until the return of *Yeshua* and the institution of the Messianic Kingdom. That little word "and" summarizes approximately 2,000 years.

It is during the Messianic Kingdom that the final phrase of verse 10 will be fulfilled, "the obedience of the nations is His." Not only will *Yeshua* reign over Israel, but He will, likewise, reign over all the nations of the world as the King of Kings and Lord of Lords.

In the words of Rabbi Munk from the Artscroll Tenach commentary:

> Until the Messiah's coming Judah will hold the royal scepter in the midst of his own nation, but the Messiah, the descendent of David will reign over the gathered nations.[145]

So Jacob has told us when the Messiah will appear—before 70AD.

At this point, Jacob moves on to describe the Messianic Kingdom itself. We now get a tiny glimpse, just a peek, at what awaits us in the future.

Conditions of the World - Genesis 49:11

> He will tether his donkey to a vine, his colt to the choicest branch; he will wash his garments in wine, his robes in the blood of grapes.

The idea being extravagantly expressed is the idea of Judah's prosperity. The pronouns "he" and "his" in verse 11 refer to Judah, as the representative of his tribe, not to the Messiah.

Remember as you read this verse that the Kingdom prosperity will not be limited to the tribe of Judah. It will extend beyond Judah to all Israel and beyond Israel to the entire world.

The donkey in biblical thinking is a symbol of peace and well being.[146] In contrast, the horse is a symbol of war. The Messiah will bring to Judah, and to the world, a reign of peace.

Vineyards and wine are symbols of prosperity and blessing.[147] In the kingdom valuable commodities will be so abundant that they can be put to common everyday use. The thrust of the imagery is that prosperity and blessing will be so plentiful that even the choicest vines will be put to such ordinary use as tethering animals. One will be able to tie a donkey to the choicest plant and be unconcerned about how much of it he has for lunch. Let him eat freely because choice vines are flourishing everywhere.

Another lavish picture closes verse 11. The picture is that wine will be so plentiful that the people of Judah can wash their clothes in it.

Verse 11 is a verse summary of the extreme and lavish abundance that will be found in the kingdom. There will be no more famines, no more poverty, and no more war. There will be only an excess of joy and fullness.

The description of the Messianic Kingdom closes in verse 12 by telling the characteristics of the people who inhabit the kingdom period.

Characteristics of the People – Genesis 49:12

> His eyes will be darker than wine, his teeth whiter
> than milk.

The pronoun "his" refers to Judah and not exclusively to the Messiah.

In verse 12, we come to rather common and unfortunate

renderings of the Hebrew. The unfortunate translation is the one used by the King James Version (KJV) and other versions such as the Jewish Publication Society (JPS) version of 1917.

The unfortunate translation used in the KJV printed in 1769 goes like this:

> His eyes *shall be* red with wine, and his teeth white with milk.

The NASB says:

> His eyes are dull from wine and his teeth white from milk.

And the JPS states:

> His eyes shall be red with wine, and his teeth white with milk.

Let us allow Rabbi Hertz to deal with these renderings. His comments come from the *Hertz Pentateuch*:

> This rendering is absurd. According to it, Judah's eyes are red from excessive drinking, and Jacob's blessing is that Judah should be a drunkard! The word rendered "red," however, means "sparkling" (Septuagint, Gunkel, Gressman); and the correct translation of the verse is: "his eyes are more sparkling than wine."[148]

The phrase compares the eyes of the people to the sparkling appearance of wine. The eyes of the people sparkle the way wine sparkles in the sun light. Their eyes are not bloodshot from drunkenness or dull from an alcoholic stupor.

In addition we have to ask this question about the final phrase of the verse, "Does drinking milk make your teeth white?" Obviously the answer is no. You do not get white teeth from drinking milk. The correct translation of the final phrase is therefore, as the NIV states it, "his teeth whiter than milk." Again, it is a comparative statement describing a healthy, flashing smile.

So what is the point of verse 12? The point of the imagery is strength and health. Everyone living in the Messianic Kingdom will be vigorous and sturdy. Illness, all the way from a cold to cancer, will be a thing of the past. Doctors and nurses and dentists and dental assistants will be out of a job. Hospitals and clinics and convalescent centers will no longer be needed. This will be life during the Messianic Kingdom.

On this glorious note of hope and promise, Jacob's message to Judah comes to its completion.

F. APPLICATION

Now for some thoughts of application.

We have seen in this section of scripture that personal character growth will determine our rewards in this world. Reuben, Simeon, and Levi all lost privileges that could have been theirs had they exhibited righteous personal character.

Our character is not something that is set in cement when we are born. Our character can change. Our character depends on our choices. The type of person that we are depends on the type of person we choose to be. What type of person do you want to be like? Do you want to be like Reuben, Simeon and Levi? Or do you want to be like Judah?

Judah was determined to grow in Godly character and surmount his character flaws. But how do you get to be like Judah?

Peter lays out the answer to that question quite clearly in 2 Peter 1:5-11.

Starting with verses 1:5-9:

> For this very reason, make every effort to add to
> your faith goodness; and to goodness, knowledge;

and to knowledge, self-control; and to self-control, perseverance; and to perseverance, godliness; and to godliness, brotherly kindness; and to brotherly kindness, love. For if you possess these qualities in increasing measure, they will keep you from being ineffective and unproductive in your knowledge of our Lord Jesus Christ. But if anyone does not have them, he is nearsighted and blind, and has forgotten that he has been cleansed from his past sins.

Peter encourages us to add to our faith in *Yeshua* character growth. This encouragement is repeated many different ways in the *Brit Chadashah*. Making the right choices leads to rewards as stated in verses 10 and 11:

Therefore, my brothers, be all the more eager to make your calling and election sure. For if you do these things, you will never fall, and you will receive a rich welcome into the eternal kingdom of our Lord and Savior Jesus Christ.

The reward of making such a choice today and everyday is a rich welcome into the eternal kingdom. Rich rewards are the results of the choice to develop Godly character.

And when will these rewards be handed out? It will happen when *Yeshua* returns to set up the Messianic Kingdom.

Matthew 16:27 tells us:

For the Son of Man is going to come in his Father's glory with his angels, and then he will reward each person according to what he has done.

When the LORD returns, will you be like Reuben, Simeon or Levi? In the kingdom, will you loose rewards that should have been yours? In the kingdom, will you be put into the background because of your sins?

Or will you be like Judah? In the Kingdom, will you be praised and rewarded, not because you are perfect, but because you chose to orient the direction of your life after God. In the kingdom will you be praised and rewarded richly because you added to your trust in *Yeshua* the choice to develop Godly character?

Our personal character growth will determine our rewards in this world and in the world to come.

END NOTES

1 Tan, Paul Lee, *Encyclopedia of 7,700 Illustrations* (Rockville, MD: Assurance Publishers, 1979), p. 991

2 "Ur" in *PC Bible Atlas for Windows*, version 1.0 (Parsons Technology, 1993)

3 Hertz, Dr. J. H., *Pentateuch and Haftorahs* (London, England: Soncino Press, 1987), p. 45

4 Pfeiffer and Harrison, eds., *Wycliffe Bible Commentary*, Logos 2.0 (Chicago, IL: Moody Press, 1962), p. 17; Douglas J. D., ed., "Babylonia" section d in *The New Bible Dictionary* (Wheaton, Illinois: Tyndale House Publishers, Inc., 1962)

5 Scherman, Rabbi Nosson, Zlotowitz, Rabbi Meir eds. *The Artscroll Tanach Series,* "Bereishis" (Brooklyn, New York: Mesorah Publications, Ltd., 1980), vol. 2, p. 424

6 Cohen, Dr. A., *Soncino Books of the Bible,* Samuel (New York, NY: The Soncino Press Ltd., 1992), p. 60

7 *Pentateuch and Haftorahs*, p. 45

8 Johnson, A. Wetherall, Bible Study Fellowship, "Genesis" (Oakland, CA: 1969), Lesson 12, p. 2

9 http://www.jewishvirtuallibrary.org/jsource/Judaism/jewpop.html

10 http://education.yahoo.com/reference/factbook/ch/popula.html

11 http://education.yahoo.com/reference/factbook/us/popula.html

12 *New International Version*, Ephesians 2:8-9

13 Henry, Matthew, *Matthew Henry's Commentary on the Whole Bible,* Logos 2.0 (Peabody, MA: Hendrickson Publishers, 1991)

14 Harris, R. L., Archer, G. L., & Waltke, B. K. (1999, c1980). *Theological Wordbook of the Old Testament* (electronic ed.). Chicago: Moody Press

15 Bible Study Fellowship, "Genesis," Lesson 12, p. 4

16 Fruchtenbaum, Dr. A., Radio Manuscript # 5, "How to Destroy the Jews" (Ariel Ministries, 1983), p. 6

17 Gaebelein, F. E., gen. ed., *Expositor's Bible Commentary* (Grand Rapids, MI: Zondervan Publishing House, 1981), vol. 3, p. 114

18 *Matthew Henry's Commentary on the Whole Bible*

19   Walvoord, John F., Zuck, Roy B., *The Bible Knowledge Commentary* (Wheaton, Illinois: Scripture Press Publications, Inc., 1985), vol.1, p. 47

20   *The Bible Knowledge Commentary*, vol.1, p. 47

21   Ibid.

22   *Pentateuch and Haftorahs*, p. 45

23   *Wycliffe Bible Commentary*, p. 17

24   Keil, C. F., Delitzsch, F., *Commentary on the Old Testament* (Grand Rapids, MI: Eerdmans Publishing Co.), vol. 1, p. 225

25   *The Artscroll Tanach Series*, "Genesis," vol. 2, p.580

26   *Biblia Hebraica Stuttgartensia* (Deutsche Biblegesellschaft Stuttgart, 1990), p. 24

27   *The Artscroll Tanach Series*, vol. 2, p. 628

28   Bible Study Fellowship, "Genesis," Lesson 17, p. 2; *Commentary on the Old Testament,* vol. 1, p. 228; Log

29   *Biblia Hebraica Stuttgartensia*, p. 24

30   *The Artscroll Tanach Series*, vol. 2, pp. 629-630; *Expositor's Bible Commentary*, vol. 2, p. 146; *Commentary on the Old Testament*, vol. 1, p. 228

31   1 Peter 4:9

32   Hebrews 13:2

33   Isaiah 58:7; Luke 14:13

34   Romans 12:20

35   *The Artscroll Tanach Series,* vol. 2, p. 638

36   2 Chronicles 20:7; Isaiah 41:8

37   Achtemier, Paul J., Th.D., *Harper's Bible Dictionary* (San Francisco: Harper and Row, Publishers, Inc., 1985), Article: Meals

38   Ibid., Logos 2.0

39   *Soncino Books of the Bible*, "The Soncino Chumash," p. 87

40   *The Bible Knowledge Commentary*, vol. 1, p. 59

41   *The Artscroll Tanach Series*, vol. 2, p. 642

42   *Expositor's Bible Commentary*, vol. 2, p. 147

43   Deuteronomy 8:4, 29:4; Joshua 3:19

44 *The Artscroll Tanach Series*, vol. 2, pp. 644-645

45 Ibid., vol. 2, p. 646

46 *The Bible Knowledge Commentary*, vol. 1, p. 59

47 *Expositor's Bible Commentary*, vol. 2, p. 148

48 *Enhanced Strong's Lexicon* (Oak Harbor, WA: Logos Research Systems, Inc., 1995)

49 *Theological Wordbook of the Old Testament*, vol. 1, p. 437

50 Bible Study Fellowship, "Genesis," Lesson 17, p. 2

51 *Commentary on the Old Testament*, vol. 1, p. 229

52 Delitzsch, Franz, *A New Commentary on Genesis Vol. II* (Edinburgh: T & T Clark), p. 84

53 *The Artscroll Tanach Series,* "Bereishis," vol. 2, p. 779

54 Ibid., p. 780

55 Bible Study Fellowship, "Genesis," Lesson 19, p. 2

56 *Biblical Commentary on the Old Testament*, p. 248

57 Ryrie, Charles C., *The Ryrie Study Bible* (Chicago: Moody Press, 1978), p. 1857

58 *The Artscroll Tanach Series,* "Bereishis," p. 784

59 Ibid., p. 782

60 *The Artscroll Tanach Series,* "Bereishis," p. 784

61 Ibid., p. 784-785

62 Ibid., p. 785

63 *The Artscroll Tanach Series,* "Bereishis," p. 785

64 *Pentateuch and Haftorahs*, p.74

65 *The Artscroll Tanach Series*, "Bereishis," p. 786

66 *Encyclopedia Judaica* (Jerusalem, Israel, Keter Publishing House Ltd., 1971), Vol. 2, Column 481

67 *The Artscroll Tanach Series,* "Bereishis," p. 789

68 Ibid.

69 Bible Study Fellowship, "Genesis," Lesson 19, p. 4

70 *A New Commentary on Genesis*, p. 86

71 *The Artscroll Tanach Series,* "Bereishis," p. 792

72   Ibid., p. 599

73   *Pentateuch and Haftorahs*, p.74

74   *The Artscroll Tanach Series,* "Bereishis," p. 797

75   Ibid., p. 798

76   *The Artscroll Tanach Series,* "Bereishis," p. 781

77   *A New Commentary on Genesis,* p. 88

78   Barnhouse, Donald G., *Genesis* (Grand Rapids: Zondervan Publishing House, 1970), p. 201

79   Bible Study Fellowship, "Genesis," Lesson 23, p. 9

80   *The Artscroll Tanach Series,* "Bereishis," p. 800

81   Ibid., p. 801

82   Ibid., p. 785

83   Ibid., p. 801

84   *Pentateuch and Haftorahs*, p.75

85   *Genesis,* p. 202

86   *The Artscroll Tanach Series,* "Bereishis," p. 803

87   Ibid, p. 803

88   *Genesis,* p. 203

89   *The Artscroll Tanach Series,* "Bereishis," p. 803

90   Ibid., p. 806

91   Ibid., p. 599

92   *Genesis,* p. 204

93   Ibid.

94   *The Artscroll Tanach Series,* "Bereishis," p. 808

95   Ibid., p. 809

96   *Genesis,* p. 205

97   Bible Study Fellowship, "Genesis," Lesson 19, p. 6

98   *Enhanced Strong's Lexicon*, (Oak Harbor, WA: Logos Research Systems, Inc., 1995

99   The word is בַּמָּקוֹם. Literally "in the place." The definite article indicates that the location is Bethel (Genesis 12:7, 13:4). The article is used when an object or a person is a well-known or

recognized fact -- Hebrew Syntax, An Outline, Second Edition, p. 18

100 *The Artscroll Tanach Series*, "Bereishis," vol. IV, p. 1223

101 Ibid., p. 1224

102 *The Artscroll Tanach Series*, "Bereishis," vol. IV, p. 1231

103 *Soncino Books of the Bible*, "Chumash," p. 165

104 *The Bible Knowledge Commentary*, Romans 11:16ff, Logos 2.0

105 *The Wycliffe Bible Commentary*, p. 32

106 Fruchtenbaum, Dr. Arnold G., *Life of the Messiah Tape Series* #3 and #4 (Ariel Ministries)

107 T*he Bible Knowledge Commentary*, John 1:48, Logos 2.0. Barclay, William, *The Gospel of John* (Philadelphia: The Westminster Press, 1955), vol. 1, p. 77

108 *Life of the Messiah Tape Series*, tapes 3-4

109 *Soncino Books of the Bible*, "Isaiah," p. 57

110 *Life of the Messiah Tape Series*, tapes 3-4; *The Bible Knowledge Commentary*, John 1:45-51, Logos 2.0

111 Roth, Cecil, Prof., Wigoder, Geoffrey, Dr., *Encyclopædia Judaica* (Jerusalem, Israel: Keter Publishing House Jerusalem, Ltd., 1972), vol. 15, col. 160

112 Ibid., vol. 15, col. 159

113 *The Bible Knowledge Commentary*, John 1:50, Logos 2.0

114 Ibid.

115 Bible Study Fellowship, "Genesis," Lesson 23, p. 9

116 Wood, D.R.W., *The New Bible Dictionary*, (Wheaton, Illinois: Tyndale House Publishers, Inc., 1962), Libronix Digital Library System 3.0

117 *The Artscroll Tanach Series*, "Bereishis/Genesis" vol. 6, pp. 2134-2138; *Commentary on the Old Testament*, vol. 1, pp. 389-390; *Expositor's Bible Commentary*, vol. 2, p. 275; *Soncino Books of the Bible*, "Chumash," pp. 302-303; *Pentateuch and Haftorahs*, pp. 183-184

118 *Pentateuch and Haftorahs*, p.184

119 *The Artscroll Tanach Series*, vol. 6, pp. 2138-2142; *Biblical Commentary on the Old Testament*, vol. 1, pp. 390-392;

Expositor's Bible Commentary, vol. 2, pg. 275-276; *Soncino Books of the Bible*, p. 303; *Pentateuch and Haftorahs*, p. 184

120 Silbermann, Rabbi A.M., *Chumash With Rashi*, Bereshit (Jerusalem, Israel: Feldheim Publishers Ltd., 1994), p. 244

121 Wood, D.R.W., and Marshall, I.H., *The New Bible Dictionary*-article "Judah" (Electric Ed., Logos 2.0)

122 Ibid.

123 Van Groningen, Gerard., *Messianic Revelation in the Old Testament* (Grand Rapids, MI: Baker Book House, 1990), p. 171

124 *The Artscroll Tanach Series*, vol. 6, p. 2152

125 Ibid., vol. 6, p. 2153

126 *Chumash with Rashi*, p. 245; *The Artscroll Tanach Series*, vol. 6, p. 2152; Fruchtenbaum, Dr. Arnold G., *Messianic Christology* (Ariel Ministries, 1998), p. 20

127 Ibid; Frydland, Rachmiel, *What the Rabbis Know About the Messiah* (Columbus, Ohio: Messianic Publishing Co. a division of Messianic Literature Outreach, 1991), pp. 16-17

128 *Soncino Books of the Bible*, p. 305

129 *The Artscroll Tanach Series*, vol. 6, p. 2152

130 *The Artscroll Tanach Series,* vol. 6, p. 2150

131 Ibid., vol. 6, p. 2153

132 Ibid.; *What the Rabbis Know About the Messiah*, p. 17

133 Yellin, Burt, *Messiah: A Rabbinic and Scriptural Viewpoint* (Denver, Co: Congregation Roeh Israel, 1984), p. 90; *What the Rabbis Know About the Messiah*, pp. 16-17

134 *What the Rabbis Know About the Messiah*, p. 17

135 Ibid.; *Messianic Christology*, p. 20

136 *The Artscroll Tanach Series*, vol.6, p. 2153

137 *Pentateuch and Haftorahs*, p. 185

138 *Commentary on the Old Testament,* vol. 1, pg. 393

139 *Messianic Revelation in the Old Testament*, p. 172

140 *Expositor's Bible Commentary*, vol. 2, pp. 279-280

141 Ibid.

142 *Messianic Christology*, p. 19; Logos 2.0, *New Bible Dictionary*, article "Shiloh"

143 *Messianic Christology*, pp. 19-20

144 Martin, Raymond., *Pugio fidei, Leipsic edition, p. 872*

145 *The Artscroll Tanach Series*, vol. 6, pp. 2153-2154

146 Ibid, vol. 6, p. 2155

147 *Expositor's Bible Commentary*, vol. 2, p. 277

148 *Pentateuch and Haftorahs*, p. 185

Robert Morris, M.Div.

Bob Morris was born October 29, 1947, in Newport, Rhode Island, the first-born son of a Jewish mother and Gentile father. He was circumcised and redeemed in accordance with Jewish law by a local rabbi. Beyond that, however, he received no spiritual training. As a teenager, he rejected his Jewishness on a religious basis and only grudgingly admitted that his heritage was Jewish.

In 1966-67, during his sophomore year at the University of Washington, he encountered genuine Christians. Due to these contacts, he received Jesus as his personal Savior when he was 19 years old. As a result of Bible studies, Bob saw that Jesus was also his promised, Holy, Jewish Messiah. At that time, he also embraced his Jewishness.

In December 1979, Bob met Arnold Fruchtenbaum, Director of Ariel Ministries, at a prophecy conference held at Bob's church. God used the Biblical message presented by Dr. Fruchtenbaum to convince Bob that he should be personally involved in presenting of Jesus the Messiah to his own Jewish people.

In May 1981, he set a new precedent by becoming Ariel's first volunteer. He established the Beth Ariel Center in Seattle, Washington and for three years saw the programs at the Center effectively disciple Jewish and Gentile believers. The Center grew to where Bob felt called to full-time service.

In September 1984, Bob and his family moved to Portland, Oregon to attend Western Conservative Baptist Seminary in order to prepare for a future staff position with Ariel Ministries. He completed a Masters of Divinity program with a concentration in Jewish ministries in the Spring of 1988.

In the fall of 1989, he planted Kehilat Ha-Mashiah (Congregation of the Messiah), a Messianic Jewish congregation in Portland, Oregon. Bob served as the Teaching Elder for the first seven years of the congregation's existence. During that time, he watched the congregation grow from 15 to 140 people in attendance and saw a steady number of Jewish people come to faith in Jesus. Concurrently, he carried out responsibilities as a Bible camp director/teacher and as a conference speaker. These ministries took him across the United States, as well as to Russia, Germany, and Israel.

In the fall of 1997, Bob and Susan moved to Southern California to become Ariel Ministries Executive Director. He reorganized the ministry, began and directed Ariel's Department of Missions and Training, and served as Field Representative.

In April 2001, Bob began another pioneering work when he became the Director of *HaDavar* Messianic Ministries in Irvine, CA. *HaDavar*'s field of service is Southern California, the second largest Jewish population center in the United States. Bob's ministry focus is primarily teaching the Bible from a Jewish perspective. He also supports outreach activities on college campuses, as well as giving training and teaching presentations and providing materials to local Messianic fellowships, Messianic congregations, and conventional churches.

About HaDavar

Our Name

HaDavar is a Hebrew term meaning "The Word." This term is found in our guiding verse, John 1:1a—"In the beginning was The Word" (in Hebrew--*Bereshit haya HaDavar*). The self-existent, creative, life-giving Word of God revealed Himself to man by becoming flesh in Jesus of Nazareth (John 1:14). Today the written Word of God is the foundation for all evangelism and discipleship; thus the basis for this ministry is *HaDavar*, the Word of God.

Our Vision

The vision of HaDavar Messianic Ministries is to glorify God and contribute to the Body of the Messiah by teaching the Bible from a Jewish perspective. This will promote personal growth as well as facilitate outreach to the Jewish community and to all of Orange County, California.

We want to encourage the Body of Messiah in Orange County to get excited about the Word of God and be stimulated by the Jewish background that permeates the entire Bible. The Jewish perspective complements Biblical studies by adding depth and color to the Bible's timeless message.

Our Goals

As God leads and provides, HaDavar Messianic Ministries will develop a Messianic Center that will be the source of:

1) a **Bible studies program** available to every Believer desiring to study the Bible from a Jewish perspective;

2) a **Jewish studies program** available to every Believer desiring studies in Jewish culture, language, history, and literature;

3) a **research library/bookstore** available to every Believer desiring quality resources for Christian and Judaic Bible study, including culture, language, history, and literature;

4) **evangelism programs** that give practical opportunities and information on how to reach the Jewish community for Messiah Jesus;

5) **networking and communication** between ministries, churches, and Messianic congregations that support HaDavar's goals; and

6) **discipleship literature** produced or distributed by HaDavar that will generate personal spiritual growth.

Other Publications by the Author

Messiah and the Tabernacle

Anti-Missionary Arguments

Comfort During Difficult Times

Biblical Perspectives on the Middle East

Who Killed Yeshua

Jewish-Christian Passover Seder

How to Share Jesus in a Jewish Way

and others.

HaDavar Classes Offered On Campus or Online at

HaDavar   YouTube

Anti-Semitism: Causes and Effects ◆ Book of Acts

Book of Ephesians ◆ Book of Genesis

Book of John ◆ Book of Psalms

Book of Revelation ◆ Greek In Plain English

How to Interpret the Bible ◆ How to Pray

Introduction to Apologetics ◆ Introduction to Scientific Apologetics

Jewish Life of the Messiah ◆ Jewish Outreach

Messiah and the Tabernacle ◆ Messianic Prophecy

Messianic Prophecies of the Tenach ◆ New Testament Overview

Old Testament Overview ◆ Psalms in Song

Prophet Daniel ◆ Prophet Ezekiel

Prophet Isaiah ◆ Prophet Jeremiah

Romans and Russians Are Coming, Oh My! ◆ Systematic Theology

The First Regathering ◆ Twelve Minor Prophets

Writings of John

Made in the USA
Las Vegas, NV
18 September 2023

77778390R00066